Contents

© Pearson Education 2004

Series editors: Martin Coles and Christine Hall

PEARSON EDUCATION LIMITED
Edinburgh Gate
Harlow
Essex CM20 2JE
England

www.longman.co.uk

First published in 2004
Second impression 2006

ISBN-10: 0-582-79643-1
ISBN-13: 978-0-582-79643-0

Photo Acknowledgements:
Jenny Alexander: David Higham Associates; Norman Hunter: Mike Herring; Rudyard Kipling: Corbis; Pratima Mitchell: David Higham Associates; Bill Naughton: Bolton Metropolitan Borough Council (Balsu Collections); Linda Newbery: John Woodward, Woodward Photographic Studio; Jean Ure: The Maggie Noach Literary Agency; with thanks also to: Anne Adeney, Louise Cooper, Griselda Gifford, Rosie McCormick, Jeremy Strong, Sean Taylor and Martin Waddell.

Printed in China
NPCC/02

The publisher's policy is to use paper manufactured from sustainable forests.

Streetwise Structure Chart

Year 5 / P6
(Ages 9-10)
Independent
Reading Stage

Adventure

Ricky, Karim and Spit Nolan (Standard) Short Stories 48 pages	Ricky, Karim and Spit Nolan (Access) Short Stories 48 pages	Stranded! Access Novel 48 pages	S.T.I.N.K. & Co. Novel 72 pages	The Secret of Monks Island Novel 96 pages

Humour

Burglars, Ducks and Kissing Frogs (Standard) Short Stories 48 pages	Burglars, Ducks and Kissing Frogs (Access) Short Stories 48 pages	Butch the Cat-Dog Access Novel 48 pages	Prince Pantyhose Novel 72 pages	Olga's Oggies Novel 96 pages

Animal

The Elephant, the Hare and the Black Cobra (Standard) Short Stories 48 pages	The Elephant, the Hare and the Black Cobra (Access) Short Stories 48 pages	The Monkey's Tale Access Novel 48 pages	Sheeka Novel 72 pages	Alligator Swamp Novel 96 pages

Year 6 / P7
(Ages 10-11+)
Independent
Plus Reading
Stage

School

Reports, Rabbits and a Beetle-teacher! (Standard) Short Stories 48 pages	Reports, Rabbits and a Beetle-teacher! (Access) Short Stories 48 pages	Callum McCoodle Access Novel 48 pages	The Time the Play Went Wrong Novel 72 pages	Over the Edge Novel 96 pages

Supernatural

The Guess, the Curse and the Message (Standard) Short Stories 48 pages	The Guess, the Curse and the Message (Access) Short Stories 48 pages	Pebbleboy Access Novel 48 pages	Tom, Sid, the Goth and the Ghost Novel 72 pages	Mapplesham Market Novel 96 pages

Historical

Through Sand, Snow and Steam (Standard) Short Stories 48 pages	Through Sand, Snow and Steam (Access) Short Stories 48 pages	Mr Darwin and the Ape Boy Access Novel 48 pages	The Match Novel 72 pages	Francis the Hero Novel 96 pages

Streetwise is the narrative fiction strand for ages 9-11 of *Literacy Land*.

The *Streetwise* stories and novels will 'hook' children into sustained and extended reading. At this point in their reading development, children are becoming independent in their choice of reading material. However, they still require help to extend their experience of the range and type of texts they read, and to discover their own preferences of authors and genres. The genre-based approach of *Streetwise* provides opportunities for children to become skilled in making these selections. *Streetwise* will help pupils to see themselves as readers who like certain types of stories and who can seek out and choose particular authors and genres.

Streetwise builds on the attraction of series reading which has always been appealing to children – from Enid Blyton's Famous Five stories to Harry Potter. Series reading can provide a hook into sustained reading, especially at a stage where readers have gained a degree of independence as readers but need to build their reading stamina. Stories in each of six genres are recognisably of the same type, so that a reader who has enjoyed one of the stories will know themselves what to read next.

Streetwise has been carefully designed to meet the reading needs of children between the ages of 9–11. The short stories are ideally suited to be taught through guided reading sessions. Guided reading sessions will provide a supported way into the 'mini-series' which is established within each genre. The novels provide excellent opportunities for reading independently or reading with the whole class.

WHAT *STREETWISE* INCLUDES:

Short story collections

The short story collections are 48 pages long. Each collection contains three stories from the same genre; two are original texts by contemporary authors, the third is a 'classic' children's story, for example by Rudyard Kipling or Richmal Crompton. The 'classic' stories are re-presented in a modern and comparative context. The inclusion of a 'classic' story within these collections is a unique feature, which allows teaching opportunities for comparing stories, for example, through discussion of plot, character, attitude change over time or language features.

Access versions of short stories

Access versions of the short story collections are simplified versions of the same text for lower attaining readers. The design and illustration is very similar to the Standard version, but the language in the Access version has been simplified to allow lower-attaining readers to read stories with an interest level above that which their reading attainment would otherwise allow. The stories have been edited and abridged to be shorter in overall length. The sentences are shorter, the language is less complex and difficult vocabulary has been simplified.

Novels

There are three novels in each of the genres – a short novel of 48 pages, one of 72 pages, and a more substantial story of 96 pages. Progression through these novels will extend children's experience of the genre and develop their reading stamina. The 48 page novel is written at Access level to allow lower attaining readers access to longer texts than might be usual for them. Children will develop their confidence by reading novels of the same length and difficulty across genres, as well as by reading novels of increasing length within each genre.

Standard and Access versions

Each *Streetwise* Short Story Collection has an Access version which provides the same content as the Standard version, but at an easier reading level. This allows pupils with different reading abilities to cover similar material in class. The covers of the books are virtually identical.

Standard version

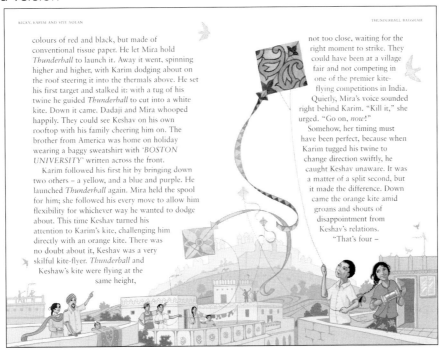

Ricky, Karim and Spit Nolan: Adventure Short Story Collection

Access version

Larger/more illustrations	Shorter, simpler sentences	Simplified vocabulary

Authorial style and content is retained	More space between lines	Increased font size

How to use this Book

Streetwise Teaching Notes provide teachers with all the information they need when planning and teaching guided, group, paired or individual reading. *Streetwise* Year 5/P6 includes short stories and novels in Adventure, Humour and Animal genres.

For each short story, there are in-depth guided reading lesson notes, which provide detailed lesson scripts and imaginative suggestions for speaking and listening and writing follow-up work. Each lesson provides question prompts for use before, during and after reading. It is envisaged that teachers will select from the questions those most appropriate to their classes. Other useful information, including the text-level focus of the lesson and a synopsis of each story, is provided at a glance.

Two pairs of guided reading lessons are provided for each short story, with each pair differentiated for both Standard and Access versions of the texts. The Access lesson follows the same objective and lesson format as the Standard lesson. Tasks and questions are modified or replaced to build differentiation into the lesson. Or, where it is more appropriate to differentiate by outcome, the task is the same in both versions, encouraging high expectations. Teachers can choose to do one or both lessons from each pair, since they follow on from one another but also stand alone as lessons in their own right. Although primarily designed for use in a guided reading session, the notes can also be used within any other reading context.

Each of the short story collections has been allocated text-level objectives from one term for the guided reading lessons notes. This is to allow comparison between the stories and support the study of the whole genre. However the texts could of course be linked to other terms and objectives. The table opposite shows how the *Streetwise* stories and novels could be linked to the NLS Range of Genre if desired.

Extending the Text
Each short story has one page of ideas for writing, drama, speaking and listening designed to support extended interaction with the text. These notes support guided, group, paired or individual reading.

Compare, Contrast and Connect
Each short story collection has a double-page spread of questions and ideas designed to trigger detailed discussion about the three stories. These notes support guided, group, paired or individual reading.

Independent/Whole Class Reading
For each novel, there are chapter-by-chapter questions, which can be used in full, or in part, to interrogate the text during both independent and whole class reading sessions. A synopsis of each novel is also provided.

Novel Ideas
Each novel has one page of ideas for writing, drama, speaking and listening designed to encourage extended interaction with the text. These notes support individual, group or whole class readingsl.

Genre Focus
Each genre has one page of question prompts and activities designed to encourage wider exploration of the genre. A list of text features provides a checklist of language, presentational and organisational devices useful when reading or writing texts within the genre.

Wider Reading
This provides synopses of further books in the same genre.

About the Author
There is an information page, which gives biographical details and information about other work, on each of the authors. Where possible, these pages have been written by the authors themselves for the *Streetwise Teaching Notes*.

NLS Genres and Objectives Covered

Story and Lesson	Text-level objective(s)
Burglars L1	Y5 T1 T3: to investigate how characters are presented, referring to the text.
Burglars L2	Y5 T1 T10: to evaluate a book by referring to details and examples in the text; Y5 T1 T12: to discuss the enduring appeal of established authors and 'classic' texts.
Duck Boy L1	Y5 T1 T3: to investigate how characters are presented, referring to the text; Y5 T1 T9: to develop an active attitude towards reading.
Duck Boy L2	Y5 T1 T2: to compare the structure of different stories; Y5 T1 T10: to evaluate a book by referring to details and examples in the text.
Kissy, Kissy L1	Y5 T1 T9: to develop an active attitude towards reading: seeking answers, anticipating events, empathising with characters and imagining events that are described.
Kissy, Kissy L2	Y5 T1 T3: to investigate how characters are presented, referring to the text; Y5 T1 T13: to record their ideas, reflections and predictions about a book, e.g. through a reading log or journal.
Spit Nolan L1	Y5 T2 T8: to investigate the treatment of different characters.
Spit Nolan L2	Y5 T2 T8: to distinguish between the author and the narrator.
Thunderball Badshah L1	Y5 T2 T2: to recognise differences of culture and place; Y5 T2 T8: to distinguish between the author and the narrator and investigate narrative viewpoint.
Thunderball Badshah L2	Y5 T2 T9: to investigate the features of different fiction genres, discussing the appeal of popular fiction.
Ricky's Wheels L1	Y5 T2 T3: to explore similarities and differences between oral and written story telling; Y5 T2 T8: to investigate the treatment of different characters.
Ricky's Wheels L2	Y5 T2 T14: to make notes of story outline as preparation for oral storytelling.
Rikki-Tikki-Tavi L1	Y5 T3 T1: to investigate a range of texts from different cultures; Y5 T3 T8: to record predictions, questions and reflections while reading, e.g. through the use of a reading journal.
Rikki-Tikki-Tavi L2	Y5 T3 T8: to record predictions, questions and reflections while reading, e.g. through the use of a reading journal; Y5 T3 T10: to write discursively about a novel or a story.
The Underwater Elephants L1	Y5 T3 T8: to record predictions, questions and reflections while reading, e.g. through the use of a reading journal.
The Underwater Elephants L2	Y5 T3 T2: to identify the point of view from which the story is told and how this affects the reader's response; Y5 T3 T3: to change point of view, e.g. tell incident or describe a situation from another point of view.
Brown Hare and the Fox L1	Y5 T3 T8: to record predictions, questions and reflections while reading, e.g. through the use of a reading journal.
Brown Hare and the Fox L2	Y5 T3 T8: to record predictions, questions and reflections while reading, e.g. through the use of a reading journal.

Year 5 NLS Range Streetwise Texts		
Term 1	Novels, stories and poems by significant children's writers	Y5 Texts: 'Burglars' and 'Duck Boy' in *Burglars, Ducks and Kissing Frogs*; *Prince Pantyhose*; 'Rikki-Tikki-Tavi' and 'Brown Hare and the Fox' in *The Elephant, the Hare and the Black Cobra*; *The Monkey's Tale*; 'Spit Nolan' in *Ricky, Karim and Spit Nolan* Y6 Texts: 'William and the School Report', 'Don't Mess with Mrs Mattock' and 'The Day I Took the Rabbit Home' in *Reports, Rabbits and a Beetle-Teacher!*; *Callum McCoodle*; *The Time the Play Went Wrong*; 'Just a Guess' in *The Guess, the Curse and the Message*; 'The Escape' and 'The Foreigner' in *Through Sand, Snow and Steam*
Term 2	Traditional stories, myths, legends fables from a range of cultures	Y5 Texts: New stories in the style of fables and traditional tales: 'Underwater Elephants' in *The Elephant, the Hare and the Black Cobra*; *Prince Pantyhose*
Term 3	Novels, stories and poems from a variety of cultures and traditions	Y5 Texts: 'Rikki-Tikki-Tavi' and 'Brown Hare and the Fox' in *The Elephant, the Hare and the Black Cobra*; 'Thunderball Badshah' in *Ricky, Karim and Spit Nolan*; Y6 Texts: 'Raising the Dead' in *The Guess, the Curse and the Message*; 'The Escape' and 'The Foreigner' in *Through Sand, Snow and Steam*; *The Match*

Streetwise and the English Language 5–14 Guidelines (Scotland)

Streetwise	Title	Reading for enjoyment	Reading to reflect on writer's ideas and craft
P6 Level C/D	Burglars, Ducks and Kissing Frogs a) Burglars	Humorous characters and situations. Cartoon/caricature style illustrations.	Identify main themes; discuss the role of character traits, e.g. forgetfulness in plot development.
	Burglars, Ducks and Kissing Frogs b) Duck Boy	Humorous characters and situations. Cartoon/caricature style illustrations.	Discuss the structure of the story, and how the outcome is reached.
	Burglars, Ducks and Kissing Frogs c) Kissy, Kissy	Humorous characters and situations. Cartoon/caricature style illustrations.	Discuss the behaviour of the characters, and the reasons for it.
	Butch the Cat-Dog	Humorous characters and situations. Cartoon/caricature style illustrations.	How are relationships between different characters presented? Why is it important to the understanding of the story?
	Prince Pantyhose	Humour of mistaken identities; unexpected version of happy ending.	How the structure and events in the story lead to the outcome. Is it a happy ending? Discuss possible alternatives.
	Olga's Oggies	Humour brought out of familiar character types and situations, with fantasy element.	Discuss how the characters' behaviour affects the story, or leads to the outcome. How does the writer influence our opinion of the characters?
	Ricky, Karim and Spit Nolan a) Spit Nolan	Adventure story related to young people's interests – go-karts.	Discuss the main aspects of character development, settings, feelings and events. How do they affect the story?
	Ricky, Karim and Spit Nolan b) Thunderball Badshah	Adventure story related to young people's interests – kite-flying.	Consider the relationship between Karim and Mira. How important is it to the story?
	Ricky, Karim and Spit Nolan c) Ricky's Wheels	Adventure story related to young people's interests – Internet use.	Consider the relationship between the two boys, using the text to illustrate.
	Stranded!	Adventure story, suspense and rescue.	Identify characters' feelings, and how they affect the story. Discuss reasons for conflict between the characters. Justify from text and own experience.
	S.T.I.N.K. & Co.	Adventure: unusual way of dealing with bullies.	Identify main themes and predict possible outcomes. Discuss likelihood of situation. Express opinions and give preferences, using text to justify.
	The Secret of Monks Island	Adventure: mystery and suspense with some historical details.	Reflect on how the structure of the story leads to the outcome; how different aspects of the plot fit together.
	The Elephant, the Hare and the Black Cobra a) Rikki-Tikki-Tavi	Short story with an animal theme: classic.	Compare the role of the animals in the three stories – as main characters or observed by others; realistic or otherwise. Identify aspects of the story which relate to the setting.
	The Elephant, the Hare and the Black Cobra b) The Underwater Elephants	Short story with an animal theme: modern version of traditional format.	Compare the role of the animals in the three stories – as main characters or observed by others; realistic or otherwise. Locate examples where the writer addresses the reader directly.
	The Elephant, the Hare and the Black Cobra c) Brown Hare and the Fox	Short story with an animal theme: family situation.	Compare the role of the animals in the three stories – as main characters or observed by others; realistic or otherwise.
	The Monkey's Tale	Animal adventure; about a pet monkey trying to survive in the wild.	Consider the situation from the different characters' points of view. Does the voice of the narrator change in different sections of the story?
	Sheeka	Adventure involving a family, a loyal dog and an earthquake.	Recognise how characters and relationships cause the situation and lead to the outcome. Understand how other themes enter and affect the plot.
	Alligator Swamp	Adventure set in South America; suspense, danger, excitement.	Identify features specifically relevant to the setting; compare with other stories in different settings.

Awareness of genre	Knowledge about language
Investigate how character description is given through text and dialogue. Compare endings.	Distinguish use of range of punctuation, including commas in direct speech. Investigate use of paragraphs.
Investigate how character description is given through text and dialogue. Compare endings.	Locate examples of connectives or adverbial phrases showing passage of time.
Identify how the humour is achieved through the frog/prince situation.	Look at how sentences are extended by connectives or embedded clauses.
Identify how the passing of time is shown. Discuss how 'flashbacks' help tell the story.	Investigate the use of conversational language in dialogue and narrative. Find examples of onomatopoeic words.
Identify how stages of the story are divided into chapters.	Understand the effect of rhetorical questions as a way of expressing views or attitudes.
Compare the opening line of each chapter, and identify how it sets the scene for what follows.	Look at how sentences are extended by connectives or embedded clauses.
Compare the stories to identify aspects of adventure common to the differing periods or settings.	Look at stylistic features of language to see how they affect the tone, e.g. repetition, passive voice, differing length of sentence.
Compare the stories to identify aspects of adventure common to the differing periods or settings.	Look at stylistic features of language to see how they affect the tone, e.g. repetition, passive voice, differing length of sentence.
Compare the stories to identify aspects of adventure common to the differing periods or settings.	Look at stylistic features of language to see how they affect the tone, e.g. repetition, passive voice, differing length of sentence.
Recognise how narrative and dialogue combine to give descriptions of character and setting.	Identify variety in verb tense and use of modal verbs. Reflect on the effect of shorter sentences to create suspense.
Recognise how narrative and dialogue combine to give descriptions of character and setting.	Identify how and why use of first person narrative affects formality of language in narrative.
Look at first and last sentences of chapters: how do they set the scene for what follows, or bring an episode to a close?	Identify adjectives and verbs selected for precise shades of meaning; suggest alternatives.
Look at and compare openings of the stories: do they set the scene for the main events quickly? How effective are the endings?	Identify adjectives and verbs selected for precise shades of meaning; suggest alternatives.
Look at and compare openings of the stories: do they set the scene for the main events quickly? How effective are the endings?	Identify adjectives and verbs selected for precise shades of meaning; suggest alternatives.
Look at and compare openings of the stories: do they set the scene for the main events quickly? How effective are the endings?	Identify adjectives and verbs selected for precise shades of meaning; suggest alternatives.
Investigate how direct speech conveys what is happening.	Investigate different sentence structures, ways of starting sentences, clauses and connectives.
Identify how diary type entries offer different viewpoints.	Recognise effect of, and justify, use of past/present tense, first/third person.
Justify how the chapter divisions fall; consider the appropriateness of the chapter titles and suggest alternatives.	Recognise use of adverbs and adverbial phrases. Examine how sentences vary to help effect.

Genre-specific text features:

central character a 'hero', risk-taker and courageous despite being in some way disadvantaged; realistic setting.

Key teaching objective:

Y5 T2 T8 … investigating … the treatment of different characters, e.g. minor characters, heroes, villains …

INTRODUCTION AND STRATEGY CHECK

- Introduce the story by providing some background information about the text. The story was first published in 1961 as part of the anthology of short stories *The Goalkeeper's Revenge and Other Stories*. 'Spit Nolan' is set in 1930s Lancashire. Has anyone heard of any other stories by Bill Naughton? Does anyone know of any stories set in that time?
- Ask one child to read aloud the first paragraph of the story. What have we learned about the main character of the story?
- Share the lesson objective with the group. Ask the children, when reading, to think about the character of Spit. How is he portrayed? What do we learn about him? As the reader, how do you feel about him? Why?
- Recall/introduce a range of reading strategies and prompts appropriate to the group. What strategies can we use to help us read and understand an unfamiliar text?

INDEPENDENT READING

- Ask the children to read independently to page 11 ('Leslie agreed. "By then," he said in a challenging tone, "I'll be able to handle her."').
- Prompt individual children to interact with the text.
  - What do you think 'slanced' means? (taken secretly)
  - Why might the children paint a motto on to their trolleys? What do the two mottoes mean?
  - After examining *The British Queen*, Spit remarks "A beautiful ball bearing race". What do you think he means? (like a perfectly tuned engine, the wheels run smoothly)

RETURNING TO THE TEXT AND RESPONSE

- Support discussion. Clarify points raised and review reading strategies.
- Discuss the character of Spit.
  - What do we learn about Spit? Justify your answer with reference to the text.
  - Spit was the leader of the gang. What evidence can you find to support this claim? (pages 5–6, 'when Spit gave the sign…'; page 6, 'Spit, the unbeaten champion, …and allow a start… '; page 11, '"Going down a steep hill," said Spit, "she should hold the road well…"')
- Discuss the character of Leslie Duckett. What type of character is Leslie Duckett? On page 8, the author writes 'He tried to edge it away…insignificant.' What do Leslie's actions tell us about his character?
- Discuss one of the 'minor' characters, for example Ernie Haddock. What are your impressions of him? What makes you think this? Refer back to page 11 ('"You've forgotten to mention one thing… A challenge race! *The British Queen* versus *Egdam*!"'). What can you deduce from what he says?
- Discuss authorial intent. Does Bill Naughton intend the reader to empathise with any of the characters? Who? In what ways does he achieve this? How successful, and in what ways, do you think Bill Naughton has been in the portrayal of Spit and Leslie so far in the story?
- Personal response. Are you keen to read on? Explain your reasons.

FOLLOW-UP

- In preparation for Lesson 2, ask the children to continue reading to page 14 ('"I'll be setting 'em off dead on the stroke of ten o'clock."')

Writing
- Ask the children to retell the story so far from the point of view of Spit.
- Alternatively, in reading journals, they could produce a labelled diagram of a trolley. Use information from pages 4 and 5 to support your interpretation.

Speaking and listening
- Form a 'Reading Circle'. Discuss what the children think makes Spit the hero of the story. How does Spit compare with heroes/heroines in other stories that you know? Generalise about what makes real and fictitious heroes/heroines and create a checklist of heroic attributes.

INTRODUCTION AND STRATEGY CHECK

- Introduce the story by providing some background information about the text. The story was first published in 1961 as part of the anthology of short stories *The Goalkeeper's Revenge and Other Stories*. 'Spit Nolan' is set in 1930s Lancashire. Has anyone heard of any other stories by Bill Naughton? Does anyone know of any stories set in that time?
- Read aloud the first two paragraphs of the story. Who is the main character? How do you know? What do we learn about him? What do you think a trolley is? What word might we use instead? (go-kart)
- Share the lesson objective with the group. Ask the children, when reading, to think about the character of Spit. How is he portrayed? What do we learn about him? As the reader, how do you feel about him? Why?
- Recall/introduce a range of reading strategies and prompts appropriate to the group. What strategies can we use to help us read and understand an unfamiliar text?

Synopsis:

A group of boys meet regularly to race their home made 'trolleys'. Spit, a sickly boy, is the champion trolley rider. Leslie has a professionally-made trolley and the two are challenged to race each other. Leslie wins the race, but it ends in tragedy as Spit is killed.

INDEPENDENT READING

- Read independently to page 10 ('Leslie agreed. "By then," he said in a challenging tone, "I'll be able to handle her."').
- Prompt individual children to interact with the text.
  - What does 'stout' mean?
  - Why did they paint on names such as *Invincible* or *Dreadnought*? What do you think these two names mean?
  - What was Cemetery Brew?
  - Why wasn't Leslie Duckett 'sure whether to feel proud or ashamed'?
  - After examining *The British Queen*, Spit remarks "A beautiful ball bearing race". What do you think he means? (like a perfectly tuned engine, the wheels run smoothly)

RETURNING TO THE TEXT AND RESPONSE

- Support discussion. Clarify points raised and review reading strategies.
- Discuss the character of Spit. What do we learn about Spit? Justify your answer with reference to the text. As the reader, how do you feel about him? Who do you predict will be the hero of the story? What makes you think this? (title, main character)
- Discuss the character of Leslie Duckett. What type of character is Leslie Duckett? How do you know? How do you think Leslie feels when he first shows his new trolley to the others? How do you think Spit feels?
- Hot seat Spit and Leslie in pairs. Ask three questions each. Respond in role.
- Personal response. Are you keen to read on? Explain your reasons.

FOLLOW-UP

- In preparation for Lesson 2, ask the children to continue reading to page 13 ('"I'll be setting 'em off dead on the stroke of ten o'clock."').

Writing

- Ask the children to imagine they are Spit. Write a diary entry describing the day's events.
- Alternatively, in reading journals, sketch and label Spit and Leslie Duckett. Use information from the text to support your interpretation.

Speaking and listening

- Form a 'Reading Circle'. Discuss what you think makes Spit the hero of the story. How does Spit compare with heroes/heroines in other stories that you know?

Spit Nolan Bill Naughton

Guided Reading Lesson 2 Standard

Genre-specific text features:

central character a 'hero', risk-taker and courageous despite being in some way disadvantaged; realistic setting.

Key teaching objective:

Y5 T2 T8 To distinguish between the author and the narrator, investigating narrative viewpoint … and perspectives on the action from different characters.

INTRODUCTION AND STRATEGY CHECK

- Recap Lesson 1 and clarify any points raised. Check that the children have read to page 14 ('"I'll be setting 'em off dead on the stroke of ten o'clock."')
- **Analyse the text. Refer back to page 12.** The author describes Leslie as wearing 'his serge Sunday suit'. What do you think he means? What is the significance of this? Spit is described as walking with 'an air of imperturbability'. What do you think this means?
- **Discuss the role of the narrator.** What 'person' is used to tell the story? (first) Who is telling the story? What evidence can you find to support your view? (e.g. page 12, 'I was pulling *Egdam* and keeping the pace easy…') Who do you think the 'I' refers to? Read out the following line on page 14: 'Leslie looked at me. "I've no objection to Bill," he said. "I know he's straight."' What does this tell us about who is telling the story? Why do you think the narrator is called Bill? **Establish that the story might be based on the author's own experiences.**
- Share the lesson objective with the group. Reiterate that the story is seen through the eyes of an observer – Spit's friend Bill. Ask the children, when reading, to jot down in their reading journals any other evidence to support this. Use page references and quotations where possible. Do you think the story might have been written differently if it had been told from Spit's point of view?
- **Recall/introduce a range of reading strategies and prompts appropriate to the group.** What strategies can we use to help us read and understand an unfamiliar text?

INDEPENDENT READING

- Ask the children to read independently to the end of the story.
- **Prompt individual children to interact with the text.** Why does the author describe the two boys as 'charioteers'? What image does this conjure up?

RETURNING TO THE TEXT AND RESPONSE

- Support discussion. Clarify points raised and review reading strategies.
- **Discuss the ending of the story.** How does the unexpected ending make you feel? Why do you think the author chose to end the story in this way? Do you think the ending is powerful? Why? On page 19, Spit says "I didn't win – I lost." Would you have felt differently if Spit had thought he had won the race? Why?
- **Review the role of the narrator and discuss different perspectives on the action.** What further evidence is there that the story is told from Bill's point of view? How do you think events might have looked from Leslie Duckett's point of view? Give examples.
- **Personal response.** Do you still regard Spit as the 'hero'? Why? Would Spit still have been regarded as a hero if he hadn't died? Would you recommend the story to anyone else? Why?

FOLLOW-UP
Writing
- **'Review and Reflect'.** In reading journals, write your own personal reflections on the text. How does the story make you feel?
- **Alternatively, assume the role of Bill.** In reading journals, write a 'farewell' letter to Spit.

Speaking and listening
- Ask the children to prepare and present a monologue by Leslie, describing events in the story.

Synopsis:

A group of boys meet regularly to race their home made 'trolleys'. Spit, a sickly boy, is the champion trolley rider. Leslie has a professionally-made trolley and the two are challenged to race each other. Leslie wins the race, but it ends in tragedy as Spit is killed.

INTRODUCTION AND STRATEGY CHECK

- Recap Lesson 1 and clarify any points raised. Check that the children have read to page 13 ('"I'll be setting 'em off dead on the stroke of ten o'clock."').
- Ask one child to summarise the story so far.
- Analyse the text. Refer back to page 11 ('Spit was in the middle of the group behind…'). At one point, Spit says "…to present you with a clout on the lug". What does he mean? What evidence can you find to suggest that Spit is very considerate of others? (pages 11–12, 'Seeing Chick's face, he said "On second thoughts…"' and '"Don't forget what day it is – folk want their sleep."')
- Discuss the role of the narrator. Who do you think is telling the story? What evidence can you find to support your view? (e.g. page 11, 'I was pulling *Egdam* and keeping the pace easy…') Who do you think the 'I' refers to? **Read out the following line from pages 12–13:** 'Leslie looked at me. "I've no objection to Bill," he said. "I know he's straight."' What does this tell us about who is telling the story? Why do you think the narrator is called Bill? Do you think the author and the narrator are the same person? Establish that the story might be based on the author's own experiences.
- Share the lesson objective with the group. Reiterate that the story is seen through the eyes of an observer – Spit's friend Bill. Ask the children, when reading, to think about how events might have looked from Spit's point of view. How do you think Spit is feeling at various points in the story?
- Recall/introduce a range of reading strategies and prompts appropriate to the group. What strategies can we use to help us read and understand an unfamiliar text?

INDEPENDENT READING

- Ask the children to read independently to the end of the story.
- Prompt individual children to interact with the text. How were Leslie and Spit going to ride their trolleys? When Spit is lying flat on his trolley, the author compares him with a bird. Why do you think this is?

RETURNING TO THE TEXT AND RESPONSE

- Support discussion. Clarify points raised and review reading strategies.
- Discuss the ending of the story. How does the ending make you feel? Did you predict such a tragic end? Why do you think the author chose to end the story in this way? Is this the type of adventure story that you are used to reading? On page 18, Spit says "I didn't win – I lost." What effect does this have upon the reader? **Refer back to page 11.** ('"I pwesent you, with the wose of the winner!" he exclaimed.') What is the significance of Chick Dale taking a yellow rose from the cemetery and giving it to Spit before the race?
- Discuss different perspectives on the action. Would any of the events have been described differently if Spit had told the story? **Hot seat Spit. Ask the children to jot down three questions to ask him. Respond in role.** Compare the questions and answers with the events as told by Bill in the story.
- Personal response. Did you enjoy reading the story? Would you recommend it to anyone else? Are you satisfied with the end of the story?

FOLLOW-UP

Writing

- 'Review and Reflect'. In reading journals, write your own personal reflections on the text. How does the story make you feel?
- Alternatively, assume the role of Bill. In reading journals, write a 'farewell' letter to Spit.

Speaking and listening

- Prepare and present a monologue by Bill, describing events in the story.

TALK FOR WRITING/DRAMA

Forum theatre

- Use the technique of 'forum theatre' to re-enact the scene when the group of children make their way to Cemetery Brew ready for the big race. The audience assist the actors playing the characters by directing the action – dialogue, gestures, movement and so on. What might Leslie be thinking on his way to Cemetery Brew? How would Spit have been walking? What might Spit have been saying to Bill?
- A possible variation is to assign each child in turn the 'remote control', which he/she can use to pause, rewind, or fast-forward the action.

Discussion

- Ask the children to imagine that Leslie is not there when Spit asks who won the race. What should Bill say? Should he do what Leslie does and lie, or should he tell Spit the truth?

Fact or opinion?

- Ask the children to use evidence from the text to decide whether the following statements are fact or opinion:
  - Bill Naughton is the narrator of the story.
  - Spit was the champion trolley-rider.
  - Leslie Duckett's family owned a pub called The British Queen.
  - Leslie's trolley, *The British Queen*, would be a stranger to him until his dying day.
- Ask the children to create their own examples.

WRITING

- Create a fictional past for Spit.
- Imagine you are a journalist for the *Cotton Pocket Daily Newspaper*. Write a newspaper report on the accident.
- Write a contemporary version of the story.
- Imagine that you are going to adapt the story for the stage.What adaptations would you need to make? For example, what props would you need? What effects would you add? Into how many scenes would you break the story? What would the actors wear?
- Write an obituary for Spit.

AUTHOR OF 'SPIT NOLAN' IN *RICKY, KARIM AND SPIT NOLAN*

Bill Naughton was born in Ireland in 1910. His family moved to England when he was four, and he grew up in Bolton in Lancashire. After he left school, he worked as a coal-bagger and driver for the Co-op and wrote during his spare time. When the Second World War broke out in 1939, he moved to London to work as a civil defence driver.

Bill Naughton's story 'Spit Nolan' comes from a collection of short stories called *The Goalkeeper's Revenge*. These stories, like Bill Naughton's other books for children, are set in the north of England in the 1920s. They are about young people's lives, friendship and sticking together when things get tough.

Bill Naughton wrote for both adults and children. He wrote plays and autobiography, as well as novels and short stories. In the 1950s, his plays began to appear on television and on the radio, and he worked in various teams of writers who produced the scripts for popular TV and radio series.

Bill Naughton loved writing and he wrote a huge amount over his lifetime. He died in 1992 on the Isle of Man, where he lived. The city of Bolton has collected Bill Naughton's papers and published work in an archive because they see him as 'a key figure in English literary life'. Among these papers are five trunks full of Bill Naughton's secret diaries: he has left instructions that these cannot be unlocked until 2015.

If you enjoyed the story Spit Nolan, you should read the other stories in *The Goalkeeper's Revenge*.

Awards
* Bill Naughton won awards for his writing of screenplays, as well as his radio plays and fiction.

Other books by Bill Naughton you might also enjoy:
* *A Dog Called Nelson*, Puffin
* *My Pal Spadger*, Puffin
* *The Goalkeeper's Revenge*, Heinemann
* *Late Night on Watling Street*, Allison & Busby

Thunderball Badshah   Pratima Mitchell

Guided Reading Lesson 1 Standard

Genre-specific text features:

hero/heroine; an element of risk; a sense of suspense; a task is accomplished.

Key teaching objectives:

Y5 T2 T2 … recognise differences of culture and place that are expressed in stories.
Y5 T2 T8 To distinguish between the author and the narrator, investigating narrative viewpoint and the treatment of different characters, e.g. minor characters, heroes, villains, and perspectives on the action from different characters.

INTRODUCTION AND STRATEGY CHECK

- Give each child a copy of the book and allow two minutes for familiarisation with the text. Ask the children to inform the group about what they have discovered. What can you tell the group about the story we are about to read? Does anyone know what 'Badshah' means? (emperor)
- Ask the children to read the first two paragraphs of the story. Where is the story set? How do you know? Establish that differences of culture and place can be seen in many stories. Can you think of another story that you have read that is about a different place or culture from your own?
- Share the lesson objectives with the group. Ask the children, when reading, to think about the setting of the story. In reading journals, they should jot down any words or phrases used which indicate the setting for the story and aspects of culture described. Does the way of life described in the story differ from your way of life? In what ways is it similar?
- Recall/introduce a range of reading strategies and prompts appropriate to the group. What strategies can we use to help us read and understand an unfamiliar text?

INDEPENDENT READING

- Ask the children to read independently to page 27 ('Tomorrow he and Mira would climb up to their rooftop … in the clear blue sky.').
- Prompt individual children to interact with the text. What do you think 'gossamer-thin scarlet silk' means? What is an 'eyrie'? What does 'a cacophony of sound' mean?

RETURNING TO THE TEXT AND RESPONSE

- Support discussion. Clarify points raised and review reading strategies.
- Review work completed in reading journals. What evidence did you find to suggest that this story is set in India? What aspects of place and culture are described? (e.g. page 26, 'Swoops of bright green parrots', 'aroma of frying bhajis', 'grandfather's camel cart', 'pompous-looking camels') Are there any similarities or differences with your own place and culture or way of life?
- Discuss the role of the narrator. What 'person' is used to tell the story? (third) How would the reader's view of events differ if a story were told in the first person?
- Discuss the character of Mira. What are your impressions of Mira? What do you know of her mother? What do you know of her grandfather?
- Personal response. Are you keen to read on? Explain your reasons.

FOLLOW-UP

- In preparation for Lesson 2, ask the children to continue reading to page 29 ('"That I share the kite-flying with you tomorrow and you take me with you to watch the planes at the airport in Delhi."').

Writing

- Ask the children to imagine they are visiting Jaipur. In reading journals, write a paragraph to describe your surroundings. Use evidence from the text to support your interpretation.
- Alternatively, write a 50-word summary of the story so far.

Speaking and listening

- Ask the children to imagine a TV programme is previewing the annual kite-flying competition. In pairs, one should assume the role of Mira, the other the role of a TV interviewer. Conduct an interview about Mira's feelings at being unable to take part in the competition.

Thunderball Badshah Pratima Mitchell

Guided Reading Lesson 1 Access

INTRODUCTION AND STRATEGY CHECK
- Give each child a copy of the book and allow two minutes in pairs for familiarisation with the text. Ask pairs of children to inform the group about what they have discovered. What can you tell the group about the story we are about to read? What did you learn from the title? Does anyone know what 'Badshah' means? (emperor) What information did you glean from the blurb? What other sources of information did you use?
- Ask one child to read aloud the first paragraph of the story. Why is Karim excited? Why do you think he has named his kite 'Thunderball the Emperor'?
- Ask another child to read aloud the second and third paragraphs of the story. Why did Karim want to win the competition so badly? Where is the story set? How do you know? Establish that differences of culture and place can be seen in many stories. Can you think of another story that you have read that is about a different place or culture from your own?
- Share the lesson objectives with the group. Ask the children, when reading, to think about the setting of the story. What images does it conjure up for you? Does the way of life described in the story differ from your way of life? In what ways is it similar?
- Recall/introduce a range of reading strategies and prompts appropriate to the group. What strategies can we use to help us read and understand an unfamiliar text?

Synopsis:
Karim is very excited about the annual kite-flying competition. His friend Mira wants to take part, but no girl has ever flown kites in the competition. She manages to persuade Karim to let her take part, and helps him to win.

INDEPENDENT READING
- Read independently to page 25 ('Tomorrow he and Mira would climb up to their rooftop...in the clear blue sky.').
- Prompt individual children to interact with the text. Why did Karim want to win the competition so badly? What would be the advantage for Keshav of 'fixing tiny balls of soft lead to his kite frame'? On page 24, Karim imagines that Thunderball will 'hover like a bird of prey'. What image does this conjure up for you?

RETURNING TO THE TEXT AND RESPONSE
- Support discussion. Clarify points raised and review reading strategies.
- Ask one child to summarise the story so far.
- Ask the children to skim read page 24 ('Karim knew he could beat that score.'). In pairs, jot down in reading journals any words or phrases used which indicate the setting for the story and aspects of place and culture described. ('tinkling rickshaw bells', 'bright green parrots', 'frying bhajis', 'grandfather's camel cart', 'pompous-looking camels', 'He came with … potatoes and onions.')
- Discuss the character of Karim. What are your impressions of Karim? What evidence do you have to support your views? How do you think he views Mira? Justify your answer with reference to the text.
- Personal response. Are you keen to read on? Explain your reasons.

FOLLOW-UP
- In preparation for Lesson 2, ask the children to continue reading to page 28 ('"That I share the kite-flying with you tomorrow and you take me with you to watch the planes at the airport in Delhi."').

Writing
- Ask the children to imagine they are visiting Jaipur. In reading journals, sketch and label your surroundings. Use evidence from the text to support your interpretation.
- Alternatively, they could retell the story so far.

Speaking and listening
- Ask the children to imagine a TV programme is previewing the annual kite-flying competition. In pairs, one should assume the role of Karim, the other the role of a TV interviewer. Conduct an interview about Karim's feelings on the eve of the competition.

Thunderball Badshah Pratima Mitchell

Guided Reading Lesson 2 Standard

Genre-specific text features:

hero/heroine; an element of risk; a sense of suspense; a task is accomplished.

Key teaching objective:

Y5 T2 T9 To investigate the features of different fiction genres, e.g. adventure, discussing the appeal of popular fiction.

INTRODUCTION AND STRATEGY CHECK

- Recap Lesson 1 and clarify any points raised. Check that the children have read to page 29 ('"That I share the kite-flying with you tomorrow and you take me with you to watch the planes at the airport in Delhi."'). Does anyone have any questions about the text so far? Can you predict what might happen next? What makes you think this?
- Establish that 'Thunderball Badshah' is classed as an adventure story. What do you think is meant by an adventure story? What features would you expect to find in an adventure story? Are any of these features present in 'Thunderball Badshah' so far?
- Share the lesson objective with the group. Ask the children, when reading, to think about what makes this an adventure story. Do you predict this will be a popular story? Why?
- Recall/introduce a range of reading strategies and prompts appropriate to the group. What strategies can we use to help us read and understand an unfamiliar text?

INDEPENDENT READING

- Read independently to the end of the story.
- Prompt individual children to interact with the text. Why did Karim not want to take Mira to Delhi with him? In Jaipur, why does everyone love the winter months? What do you think 'thermals' are? How do you know? In what ways do both Karim and Mira take risks?

RETURNING TO THE TEXT AND RESPONSE

- Support discussion. Clarify points raised and review reading strategies.
- Ask one child to summarise the story. Can anyone add anything? Does this story remind you of any stories you have read before?
- Discuss the genre. In your opinion, what makes 'Thunderball Badshah' an adventure story? Ask the children, in pairs, to create a checklist of 'Adventure Story Features'. Is 'Thunderball Badshah' a typical adventure story? Does the fact that 'Thunderball Badshah' is a short story affect the style and type of adventure that it is?
- Discuss what 'popular fiction' is. What is meant by the term 'popular fiction'? (fiction designed to appeal to the majority of people, sometimes regarded as 'light' reading) What do you think makes good popular fiction? What makes a book popular? In your view, would 'Thunderball Badshah' deserve the stamp of 'popular fiction'? Can classic fiction be popular fiction? Have you read any popular fiction?

FOLLOW-UP

Writing

- Ask the children to imagine that they have been asked to review 'Thunderball Badshah' for the section of their school magazine entitled 'Read or Reject'. Write a review of the story drawing comparisons with other popular fiction you have read.
- Alternatively, write another adventure short story. Use the checklist of 'Adventure Story Features' as a reference point.

Speaking and listening

- In pairs, ask the children to discuss whether 'Thunderball Badshah' should be classed as popular fiction. Rate the story on a scale of 1–10 and give reasons to justify your rating. Compare your views with those of another pair.

INTRODUCTION AND STRATEGY CHECK

- Recap Lesson 1 and clarify any points raised. Check that the children have read to page 28 ('"That I share the kite-flying with you tomorrow and you take me with you to watch the planes at the airport in Delhi."').
- Ask one child to summarise the story so far. Can you predict what might happen next? What makes you think this?
- Establish that 'Thunderball Badshah' is classed as an adventure story. What do you think is meant by an adventure story? To what degree would you say that 'Thunderball Badshah' is an adventure story?
- Share the lesson objective with the group. Ask the children, when reading, to think about what makes this an adventure story. Did you enjoy the story? Why?
- Recall/introduce a range of reading strategies and prompts appropriate to the group. What strategies can we use to help us read and understand an unfamiliar text?

INDEPENDENT READING

- Ask the children to read independently to the end of the story.
- Prompt individual children to interact with the text. Why did Karim not want to take Mira to Delhi with him? What persuaded him to change his mind? Where did the competition take place? In Jaipur, why does everyone love the winter months? How did Karim bring down Keshav's kite? Do you think Karim is very competitive? What makes you think this?

RETURNING TO THE TEXT AND RESPONSE

- Support discussion. Clarify points raised and review reading strategies.
- Ask the children, in pairs, to summarise the story. Does this story remind you of any other stories you have read before?
- Discuss the genre. In your opinion, what makes 'Thunderball Badshah' an adventure story? As a group, compile a checklist of 'Adventure Story Features'. Thinking about any other adventure stories you have read, can you add any other features to the checklist? Is 'Thunderball Badshah' a typical adventure story? Why?
- Discuss what 'popular fiction' is. What is meant by the term 'popular fiction'? (fiction designed to appeal to the majority of people, sometimes regarded as 'light' reading) What makes a book popular? In your view, would 'Thunderball Badshah' deserve the stamp of 'popular fiction'? Have you read any other examples of popular fiction?

FOLLOW-UP

Writing

- Ask the children to design a poster advertising Jaipur's kite-flying competition.
- Alternatively, they could write another short story adventure for Karim and Mira.

Speaking and listening

- Form a 'Reading Circle'. Discuss whether 'Thunderball Badshah' should be classed as popular fiction. Rate the story on a scale of 1–10 and give reasons to justify your rating. Compare your views with those of another group.

Synopsis:
Karim is very excited about the annual kite-flying competition. His friend Mira wants to take part, but no girls have ever flown kites in the competition. She manages to persuade Karim into letting her take part, and helps him to win.

TALK FOR WRITING/DRAMA

Thought tracking

- Freeze-frame key incidents of the story and use the technique of thought tracking to reveal the character's thoughts at various points in the drama:
  - What might Karim have been thinking as he assembled his kite?
  - What might Mira have been thinking as she watched Karim assemble his kite?
  - What might Mira have been thinking when she heard the clunk-clunk of camel bells sounding to signal the arrival of Dadaji, her grandfather?
  - What might Karim have been thinking as the gunshot went off marking the start of the competition?

Debate

- Karim is embarrassed to have Mira as a friend. Is he right to be embarrassed?

Hypothetical happenings

- Discuss 'What ifs'. Ask the children to create their own 'what if' examples.
  - What if Mira hadn't told Karim what Keshav was doing with his kite?
  - What if a freak wind hadn't caught Karim's kite and blown it into the very top branches of the guava tree?
  - What if Mira's grandfather hadn't arrived until the following day?
  - What if Keshav had won the competition?
- Ask the children to create their own 'What if' examples.

WRITING

- Design a questionnaire to put to the author. Swap with a partner and respond as the author.
- Write a letter from Mira to her grandfather either before or after the competition.
- Design and write a programme for spectators of the kite-flying competition. Include profiles of the competitors, a form guide and a run-down on the kites.
- Imagine that the kite did not get stuck in the top branches of the guava tree. Write an alternative ending.
- Retell the story from the point of view of Mira.

About the Author

AUTHOR OF 'THUNDERBALL BADSHAH' IN *RICKY, KARIM AND SPIT NOLAN* AND *SHEEKA*

I was born in India and went to universities in Delhi, London and the United States. India is a great inspiration for many of my stories. I go there at least twice a year, to visit my family in New Delhi and to visit other parts of the country.

My story 'Thunderball Badshah' is based in Jaipur, a city I visited recently, where kite-flying is very popular. Kite-flying is a very traditional sport and was always very much a boy's sport when I was growing up. It is very popular in inner cities where rooftops are a substitute for recreation grounds.

When writing this story, I referred to my familiarity with the streets and bazaars of Jaipur and my memories of kite-flying festivals (which usually take place in spring) in order to bring the story and its characters to life.

When I wrote *Sheeka*, I wanted to get away from the authorial voice and didn't want to impose myself on the reader for a change. Deciding to have a 'dog mind' as one of the narrators came to me quite naturally, as I feel that animals (especially intelligent dogs) have thought processes and feelings, even though they don't use human language to express themselves.

I have always loved reading and used to read about six books a week when I was growing up. I have four books on the go at the moment, but when I am on holiday I do my childhood thing and gallop through a book a day!

If you enjoyed reading 'Thunderball Badshah' and *Sheeka*, one of my latest titles could interest you: *The Guru's Family* is set in Coventry and a village in the Punjab.

Awards
- *Dadijan's Carrot Halvah* was listed in Children's Books of the Year 1988.

Other books by Pratima Mitchell you might also enjoy:
- *The Guru's Family,* Hodder Wayland
- *Two Asian Tales, Literacy Land,* Longman
- *Magical Stories from India, Pelican Guided Reading and Writing,* Longman
- *The Tale of a Turban,* Oxford University Press
- *Dance of Shiva,* Hamish Hamilton
- *Dadijan's Carrot Halvah,* Hamish Hamilton

Pratima Mitchell also writes for the *Genre Range* strand of *Literacy Land*, the *Longman Book Project* and *Pelican Guided Reading and Writing*.

Ricky's Wheels Jenny Alexander

Guided Reading Lesson 1 Standard

Genre-specific text features:

central characters are 'heroes', one character courageous despite being in some way disadvantaged; realistic setting.

Key teaching objectives:

Y5 T2 T3 To explore similarities and differences between oral and written story telling.
Y5 T2 T8 To distinguish between the author and the narrator, investigating narrative viewpoint and the treatment of different characters, e.g. minor characters, heroes, villains, and perspectives on the action from different characters.

INTRODUCTION AND STRATEGY CHECK

- Ask the children to read the blurb independently. What type of story are you about to read? What leads you to this conclusion?
- Ask one child to read aloud the first three paragraphs of the story. What have we learned about the two main characters? What 'person' is used to tell the story? (first) How do you know? What do we know about the narrator?
- Share the lesson objectives with the group. Ask the children, when reading, to think about the role of the narrator, and the differences between writing a story and telling a story. In what ways does telling the story in the first person affect the reader's view of events? In what ways might 'Ricky's Wheels' change if it were being told orally?
- Recall/introduce a range of reading strategies and prompts appropriate to the group. What strategies can we use to help us read and understand an unfamiliar text?

INDEPENDENT READING

- Ask the children to read independently to page 41 ('I shrugged. "Let's go to her list of contacts and see if we can work it out."').
- Prompt individual children to interact with the text. How did the well-meaning person spoil the race? What is Sam's relationship like with his sister Abbie? Can you predict what will happen in the rest of the story?

RETURNING TO THE TEXT AND RESPONSE

- Support discussion. Clarify points raised and review reading strategies.
- Discuss the role of the narrator. Who is the narrator of the story? What evidence can you find to justify your answer? (page 39, 'When I got to the Carlton Street gate he was waiting for me. "Hard cheese, Sam!" he said, grinning.') In what ways do you think events would be different if told from Ricky's point of view?
- Discuss the character of the narrator – Sam. What do you know about him?
- Ask the children in pairs to retell the story so far. What are the differences between a spoken story and a written story? What did you have to do to tell this story? (Oral storytelling requires expression, intonation; relies on gestures, pauses, facial expression, body language; is more spontaneous. Written language requires the use of punctuation, paragraphs, complete sentences; is planned.) Was it easy to remember the order of events? Could you remember specific details about the characters? What would prompt you to remember? Establish that, like writing, telling a known story generally requires careful planning and thought.
- Personal response. Are you keen to read on? Explain your reasons.

FOLLOW-UP

- In preparation for Lesson 2, ask the children to continue reading to page 43 ('"If it takes you fifteen minutes, I bet I can do it in ten."').

Writing

- Ask the children to retell the story so far from the point of view of Ricky. Are there any advantages to having two different perspectives on the same action?
- Alternatively, create a fictional account of the first meeting between Ricky and Sam. When did they become friends? How did Ricky have his accident?

Speaking and listening

- Different perspectives. In pairs, imagine one of you is one of the well-meaning passers-by that spoils Ricky and Sam's race. Describe events as you see them and give reasons for your actions. Your partner must challenge you and question your view of events.

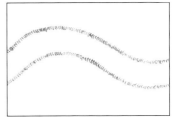

Synopsis:

The best of friends, Ricky and Sam enjoy racing each other. One day, they read Sam's sister's messages and become convinced that she is meeting someone suspicious. As it turns out, she is simply meeting her boyfriend.

INTRODUCTION AND STRATEGY CHECK

- **Ask a child to read aloud the blurb.** What type of story are you about to read? What leads you to this conclusion?
- **Read aloud the first three paragraphs of the story.** What have we learned about the two main characters? What do we know about who is telling the story?
- **Share the lesson objectives with the group.** Ask the children, when reading, to think about the character telling the story – the 'me' in the phrase 'Ricky and me' in the second line of the story – and the differences between writing a story and telling a story. What do we learn about the narrator? What does he think of Ricky? In what ways might 'Ricky's Wheels' change if it were being told orally?
- **Recall/introduce a range of reading strategies and prompts appropriate to the group.** What strategies can we use to help us read and understand an unfamiliar text?

INDEPENDENT READING

- **Ask the children to read independently to page 40** ('I shrugged. "Let's go to her list of contacts and see if we can work it out."').
- **Prompt individual children to interact with the text.** On page 37, why does the old woman say "You should be ashamed of yourself, young man! What about your friend?" On page 38, the narrator states that his sister 'thinks she's cool' and 'talks down to me quite a lot'. Why doesn't he mind this? Can you predict what will happen in the rest of the story? What makes you think this?

RETURNING TO THE TEXT AND RESPONSE

- Support discussion. Clarify points raised and review reading strategies.
- **Discuss the role of the narrator.** Who is the narrator of the story? How do you know? Refer to page 37, 'When I got to the Carlton Street gate he was waiting for me. "Hard cheese, Sam!" he said, grinning.' **Establish that the story is told from the point of view of Sam.** Do you think the story might have been different if told from Ricky's point of view? Why?
- **Orally retell the story to the group.** What are the differences between a spoken story and a written story? What did I have to do to *tell* the story? (Oral storytelling requires expression, intonation; relies on gestures, pauses, facial expression, body language; is more spontaneous. Written language requires the use of punctuation, paragraphs, complete sentences; is planned.) **Establish that, like writing, telling a known story generally requires careful planning and thought.**
- **Personal response.** Are you keen to read on? Explain your reasons.

FOLLOW-UP

- In preparation for Lesson 2, ask the children to continue reading to the end of page 41 ('"If it takes you fifteen minutes, I bet I can do it in ten."').

Writing

- In reading journals, ask the children to list five facts about Ricky and five facts about Sam. Use quotations and page references to support your answers.
- Alternatively, create a fictional account of the first meeting between Ricky and Sam. When did they become friends? How did Ricky have his accident?

Speaking and listening

- Ask the children to imagine they are the well-meaning passer-by who passes judgement on Sam. Describe events as you see them and give reasons for your actions.

Ricky's Wheels   Jenny Alexander

Guided Reading   Lesson 2   Standard

Genre-specific text features:

central characters are 'heroes', one character courageous despite being in some way disadvantaged; realistic setting.

Key teaching objective:

Y5 T2 T14 To make notes of story outline as preparation for oral storytelling.

INTRODUCTION AND STRATEGY CHECK

- Recap Lesson 1 and clarify any points raised. Check that the children have read up to page 43 ('"If it takes you fifteen minutes, I bet I can do it in ten."'). What do you predict will happen in the rest of the story? Do you think Ricky will get there before Sam? What leads you to this conclusion?
- In reading journals, ask the children to make a list of the key events in the story so far. This will serve as a prompt for telling the story orally later on.
- Share the lesson objective with the group. Ask the children, when reading, to complete their lists, noting down the key events in the rest of the story. Include any other details that would support the retelling of the story, for example the introduction of a new character, character's actions and character's responses to particular events.
- Recall/introduce a range of reading strategies and prompts appropriate to the group. What strategies can we use to help us read and understand an unfamiliar text?

INDEPENDENT READING

- Read independently to the end of the story.
- Prompt individual children to interact with the text. How do you think Sam is feeling at various points? What evidence can you find to support your view? How would you feel if your brother or sister had done something similar? Do you think Sam had subconsciously been letting Ricky win when they raced through the park? What makes you think this? In your view, what makes this an adventure story? Can you pick out any features that are typical of an adventure story?

RETURNING TO THE TEXT AND RESPONSE

- Support discussion. Clarify points raised and review reading strategies.
- Review work completed in reading journals. Ask the children, in pairs, to compare their lists and make any necessary changes. Ask one child to read out the list of the key events in the story and any other further details recorded.
- Personal response. Why do you think the author has chosen a contemporary setting for the story? In what ways does this make the story more appealing to some children? In what ways do the issues raised make the story more appealing to some children? Do you prefer to read more modern stories or do you enjoy reading a mixture of both modern and traditional stories?

FOLLOW-UP

Writing

- Ask the children to write an e-mail from Abbie to one of her friends explaining what has happened and how she feels. Use a colloquial style like that used by Abbie in the story.
- Ask the children to write another adventure for Sam and Ricky set in a different time. Choose to set your story in, for example, Victorian times, the future or during The Second World War.

Speaking and listening

- Use notes to rehearse and present for an audience an oral rendition of the story. The audience may 'pause' your story and ask you questions along the way. What was Ricky thinking when…? What did Abbie say to Jason after Ricky and Sam left them at the gardens?

INTRODUCTION AND STRATEGY CHECK

- Recap Lesson 1 and clarify any points raised. Check that the children have read to page 41 ('"If it takes you fifteen minutes, I bet I can do it in ten."').
- Generate discussion about the text so far.
  - On pages 39 and 40 we are shown Abbie's Net Messenger page. What do you notice about the language she uses to communicate with her friends? Why is it appropriate for this purpose? When would it be inappropriate? Why?
  - What do you predict will happen in the rest of the story? Do you think Ricky will get there before Sam? What leads you to this conclusion?
- Ask the children as a group to jot down the main events in the story so far. List them in chronological order. These will serve as a prompt for telling the story later on.
- Share the lesson objective with the group. Ask the children, when reading, to think about the key events in the rest of the story.
- Recall/introduce a range of reading strategies and prompts appropriate to the group. What strategies can we use to help us read and understand an unfamiliar text?

INDEPENDENT READING

- Ask the children to read independently to the end of the story.
- Prompt individual children to interact with the text. How do you think Sam is feeling at various points? What evidence can you find to support your view? How would you feel if your brother or sister had done something similar? What is the 'Cut'? Why didn't Abbie tell Sam about her new boyfriend Jason? On the way home, why was Ricky cross with Sam?

RETURNING TO THE TEXT AND RESPONSE

- Support discussion. Clarify points raised and review reading strategies.
- Ask the children, in pairs, to summarise what happened in the rest of the story. As a group, they should complete the list of main events in the story.
- Personal response. Did you enjoy reading the story? Would you recommend it to anyone else? Why? What other adventure stories have you read? Is 'Ricky's Wheels' the type of adventure story you have read before? What do you think makes this story an adventure?

FOLLOW-UP

Writing

- Ask the children to write an email from Sam to Ricky explaining what happened after Abbie returned home.
- Alternatively, write another adventure for Sam and Ricky.

Speaking and listening

- Using the group notes, ask the children to rehearse and present for an audience, in pairs or as a group, an oral rendition of the story. The audience may 'pause' their story and ask them questions along the way. What was Ricky thinking when…? What did Abbie say to Jason after Ricky and Sam left them at the gardens?

Synopsis:
The best of friends, Ricky and Sam enjoy racing each other. One day, they read Sam's sister's messages and become convinced that she is meeting someone suspicious. As it turns out, she is simply meeting her boyfriend.

TALK FOR WRITING/DRAMA

Mantle of the expert

- Dramatise the story. Prior to the session, ask a group of children to prepare a list of the DOs and DON'Ts of Internet safety. Using the technique of 'Mantle of the expert', the children present their findings to an audience at an appropriate point in the drama.

Debate

- Ricky and Sam had every right to look on Abbie's 'Net Messenger' and run after her to the café. What do you think?

Quote unquote

- Locate and discuss examples from the text which demonstrate:
  - that Ricky and Sam are the best of friends
  - that Ricky is very independent
  - that Ricky enjoyed racing Sam
  - that the story is set in a contemporary setting.

WRITING

- Imagine you are Abbie. Write a text message to Jason the following day.
- Devise and label a story map illustrating the route taken by Ricky and Sam to find Abbie.
- Write another adventure story based on a race.
- Retell the story from the point of view of Abbie.
- Which part of the story did you find most gripping? Create a storyboard of the scene to show how the action develops.

Jenny Alexander

About the Author

AUTHOR OF 'RICKY'S WHEELS' IN *RICKY, KARIM AND SPIT NOLAN* AND *STRANDED!*

I really enjoyed writing my *Streetwise* stories because it involved a perfect mix of interesting research, happy memories and making things up.

I used the Internet to research my story, 'Ricky's Wheels'. I found a writer called Gary Karp, who has been in a wheelchair since his teens. I read his book, *Life on Wheels* and emailed him with questions I still had about what Ricky would be able to do and how he would do it. In my original idea, Sam was going to push Ricky up the hills and jump on the back of his wheelchair as they were both coming down. However, Gary told me that that wouldn't work because the wheelchair would overbalance, and anyway Ricky would be perfectly capable of wheeling uphill on his own. When I had finished the story, Gary read it for me to make sure it was believable.

The idea for *Stranded!* came from my own childhood, when my family had a caravan on Hayling Island very close to a muddy creek. One time, my sister and our cousin tried to cross the creek, but the mud in the middle was much deeper than they had expected. Then we noticed the tide was coming in … It was absolutely terrifying!

I haven't been back to Hayling Island since I was eight, so I decided to set the story on the Norfolk coast, which I've visited more recently. I read about salt marshes on the Internet to refresh my memories before I started writing.

I love reading and writing. I don't enjoy writing or reading long passages of description because I'm quite an impatient person. I'm also rather reckless, so I tend to jump in with both feet – and then panic! I guess that's why my characters often have to find ways of overcoming fear and solving problems.

If you have enjoyed reading 'Ricky's Wheels' and *Stranded!* you might also like *Pedal Power: Land's End to John o' Groats* as it has lots of geography in a short diary format, which could give you some ideas for settings when you are writing stories of your own.

Awards
* *Pedal Power: Lands End to John o'Groats* was selected for the Child Education and Junior Education 'Best Books in 2002' supplement.

Other books by Jenny Alexander you might also enjoy:
* *Haunting for Beginners*, Puffin
* *The Good Ghost Guide, Pelican Hilo*, Longman
* *Pedal Power: Land's End to John o'Groats, Info Trail*, Longman
* *Bullies, Bigmouths and So-Called Friends*, Hodder

Jenny Alexander also writes for the *Story Street, Genre Range* and *Info Trail* strands of *Literacy Land* and *Pelican Hilos*.

STYLES AND TECHNIQUES

Setting

The settings in the three adventure short stories are in stark contrast to one another: 1930s Lancashire, Jaipur in India and contemporary life in a small British town.

Writing

- Ask the children to list the features of the three settings. Use an extended Venn diagram to show which aspects of setting are similar and which are different.

Narrative voice

- In two of the short stories, first person narration is used: 'Spit Nolan' and 'Ricky's Wheels'. Compare and contrast the effects of the narration in these two stories with 'Thunderball Badshah', which is narrated using the third person.
- Discuss why writers use the first person. Why do you think Bill Naughton and Jenny Alexander opted for first person narration? In their stories, what effect does this have on the reader? Is it more powerful to write using the first person? As the reader, do you empathise more when a story is told in the first person? When are you more likely to get an objective view of events? Why? Is first person narration more likely to be used when the author is basing the story upon his or her own experiences?

Writing

- Retell 'Thunderball Badshah' using first person narration from the point of view of Mira. Do events look different? What is the effect on the reader?

THEMES

Friendship

- For the most part, all three of the short stories involve adult-free groups of children. The adventures are seen through the eyes of children: Spit Nolan and Bill, Ricky and Sam, and Karim and Mira. Compare and contrast the theme of friendship in all three of the short stories.
- Contrast the friendship demonstrated by Spit with the friendship demonstrated by Karim. How do the two characters display their feelings towards their friends?
- Compare and contrast the qualities of friendship displayed by Bill, Ricky and Mira. Who would you rather have as a friend? Why?

Writing

- Ask the children to choose one of the characters and explain why they would like them as a friend. Use evidence from the text to support your answer. What qualities do you consider important in a friendship?
- Ask the children to choose three characters from any of the three stories. What qualities of friendship are displayed by these characters? What can you infer about their commitment to friendship?

CHARACTERS

- Compare the three main characters: Spit, Ricky and Karim. In what ways are they similar? (disadvantaged, boys, risk-takers) Whom do you admire most? Why?
- Compare Abbie and Mira. How are they similar? How do they behave towards Ricky and Karim?

Compare, Contrast and Connect

CLASSIC VERSUS CONTEMPORARY

Use of language

- Ask the children to investigate the differences in language use across two of the texts. For example, 'Spit Nolan' includes examples of Lancashire dialect and 'Ricky's Wheels' includes examples of colloquial language.
- Discuss the following with reference to the texts:
  - When is it appropriate to use colloquial language?
  - Why has Bill Naughton chosen to include examples of dialect?
  - When is it appropriate to use more formal language?
  - Why might we sometimes abbreviate words, as Abbie does?

Writing

- Ask the children to find and list examples of colloquial language and dialect used in 'Spit Nolan': for example, '…he never came a cropper.', '"Hey, chaps, wot's Leslie got?"', '"I'll be setting 'em off dead…"' and '"Tha just licked me. Eh, Bill?"'.
- Ask the children to find and list examples of modern colloquial language used in 'Ricky's Wheels': for example, 'wanna meet me, then?', 'bus leaves in 5. cu soon' and 'betta not'.

Customs

- Ask the children to find examples of differences in pastimes across the two texts: for example, 'Spit Nolan' refers to 'trolley-rider', 'Sunday suit' and 'charabanc', and 'Ricky's Wheels' refers to 'computers', 'Road Race', 'Net Messenger' and 'the café at the canal centre'.
- Discuss how and why pastimes change over time. What do you like to do?

PERSONAL RESPONSE

- Ask the children to choose a scene from one of the stories that they think is particularly effective. Dramatise and present for an audience, and explain your reasons for choosing this scene.

Synopsis:

Joe is unhappy that his 'towny' cousins Clare and Peter are coming to stay for ten days. His mother decides that he and his sister Vicky should entertain them by taking them out for a bike ride. They decide to ride down to the salt marshes by the sea. Clare and Peter ignore Joe's advice and are stranded by the incoming tide. Joe seeks help, and his cousins are rescued along with Vicky, who has also fallen into the marshes.

TWENTY QUESTIONS

Chapter 1	In what ways does this story so far remind you of others that you have read?
Chapter 1	Why do you think Joe is not very enthusiastic when he hears that Clare and Peter are coming to stay?
Chapter 1	What are your first impressions of Vicky? What role do you think she might play in the story?
Chapter 1	How would you describe the house where Joe and Vicky live with their mother?
Chapter 1	What do you imagine Car Boot Creek to be? Why?
Chapter 2	How does Joe's view of Clare and Peter change and evolve during the second chapter?
Chapter 2	Why do you think Vicky tries to impress Clare and Peter?
Chapter 2	Predict what you think will happen next. How do you think the story will end?
Chapter 3	At the beginning of Chapter 3, we see Clare and Peter ignoring Joe's advice. Why do you think they do this?
Chapter 3	Imagine you are Clare. What is going through your mind as you start to sink into the mud?
Chapter 3	What would you have done if you were in Joe's place in this chapter?
Chapter 4	Why do you think Tinks is barking so furiously during this chapter?
Chapter 4	What could Joe have done next, if the man and woman in the house had not been at home?
Chapter 5	Vicky's body, when it is dragged into the boat, is described as being 'as limp as a dishrag'. What does this mean? What does it signify?
Chapter 5	Consider the role of Tinks in the story so far. How would you describe her actions?
Chapter 6	At the beginning of the final chapter, why do you think Joe prefers to stay with Vicky rather than keep Clare and Peter company?
Chapter 6	Do you agree with Joe, that it isn't fair for him to take all the blame? Why?
Chapter 6	What does Joe mean when he says the coast road 'wasn't exactly a motorway'?
Chapter 6	Describe how Joe's mother's view of the situation changes during the final chapter.
Chapter 6	How has Joe's attitude to Clare and Peter changed by the end of the story? Why?
Overview	In what ways does the author create a sense of tension?

Novel Ideas

TALK FOR WRITING/DRAMA

If using the text with a group or as a class novel

- **Freeze-frame.** Retell through drama one or more chapters of the story. Perform for an audience and freeze-frame key incidents: for example, when they all decide to go to Car Boot Creek, or when the tide starts to come in. Record the still images on digital camera and capture onto presentation software such as PowerPoint to create an electronic storyboard. Use as a tool for organising writing.
- **Oral storytelling.** Retell the story around the group or the class, each child in turn adding two sentences.
- **Debate.** Joe's and Vicky's 'village' life is better than Clare and Peter's 'town' life. What do you think?
- **Hypothetical happenings.** Discuss 'What ifs':
  - What if Auntie Jean and Uncle Simon had stayed at Carter's Yard?
  - What if Joe's mum had known about Car Boot Creek?
  - What if Vicky hadn't tried to impress Clare and Peter at Car Boot Creek?
  - What if no one had been in the house where Joe went to get help?
  - What if…? (Create your own examples.)

RESPONSE TO THE TEXT

As ongoing work in reading journals

- Imagine you are Clare or Peter. Write a diary entry describing your first day with Joe and Vicky at Carter's Yard. At the end of the story, write a diary entry describing your second day with Joe and Vicky. Contrast the two entries. Do the same from the point of view of Joe or Vicky and compare their different perspectives of events.
- Imagine the setting for the story. Sketch a map of Umberly, Cold Clayton and the coast road. Use information from the text and include a key.
- Imagine the telephone call between Joe and his mum at the end of the story. Write a transcript of the call.
- Have you ever been stranded? Write an anecdotal account of your experience.
- Imagine you are the Safety Officer for Cold Clayton District Council. After hearing about the incident at the salt marshes, you realise that the area urgently needs a warning notice. Compile a list of rules and regulations about safety at the salt marshes.
- Imagine that the incident is reported on Cold Clayton local radio. Write and present the script for a report on the news bulletin.

Independent / Whole Class Reading

Synopsis:

Owen joins up with Stevie Trovato and his 'associates', Stumpy and Amy, to form the vigilante group S.T.I.N.K. & Co. Their first assignment involves sneaking into the ice cream van belonging to Stevie's father. Everything is going well, until Stevie decides to climb into the driver's seat – he is seen by his headteacher Mr Thorn, who assumes that the ice cream van has been stolen and drives it back to the Trovatos' house. However, S.T.I.N.K. & Co. still manage to complete their assignment.

TWENTY QUESTIONS

Chapter 1	Why do you think Owen has chosen to join S.T.I.N.K. & Co.?
Chapter 1	Consider what we learn about the character of Stevie in this chapter. How would you describe him? What characters from other books, films or TV programmes does he remind you of?
Chapter 1	Why do you think Stevie insists that all the 'agents' wear black and speak with an American accent?
Chapter 1	Why is Stevie so anxious to say that Amy is wrong when she says that S.T.I.N.K. & Co. are 'kind of like gangsters'? How *are* they like gangsters? How are they different?
Chapter 1	What do you think the four agents are going to do when they 'pay Shane Maxwell a little visit'?
Chapter 2	Consider the character of Stumpy. What are his distinctive characteristics? Based on these, what do we expect his role to be in the adventure?
Chapter 2	Describe Stevie's plan for the visit to Shane Maxwell. Do you think his plan will work? What could go wrong?
Chapter 2	Consider the role of humour in the story so far. In what ways is the story funny? Do you think it is *meant* to be funny?
Chapter 3	Why do you think Stumpy and Owen refuse to stand under Amy's umbrella?
Chapter 3	On page 29, the author writes: 'Even in the middle of winter he could be seen selling frozen treats dressed only in a white T-shirt and beige cotton trousers.' Why do you think Mr Trovato acts in this way?
Chapter 3	What do we find out about Mr Thorn in Chapter 3? What words could we use to describe him?
Chapter 3	Read the sequence on pages 33–35, where Mr Thorn is driving the ice cream van, and imagine you were watching it on a film or TV programme. How do you think the episode would be portrayed? How do you think you would feel as you watched it?
Chapter 3	Compare and contrast the behaviour of Stevie and Owen in this chapter. How does it differ?
Chapter 4	Do you think Mr Trovato believes the story that Stevie tells about his friends wanting to drive ice cream vans? Why?
Chapter 4	How does Owen's father react when he arrives? What do you think his view of the situation is? How do you think his mother will react when Owen gets home?
Chapter 5	Why is it predictable that Owen is the last agent to arrive at the sandpit?
Chapter 5	Why do you think Shane Maxwell has 'stopped bothering' Nigel? Does it surprise you that Stevie's plan has seemed to work? Why?
Chapter 5	Why do you think the idea of S.T.I.N.K. & Co. T-shirts is 'beginning to grow' on Owen?
Chapter 5	Does the world become 'a much more interesting place' with people like Stevie, Stumpy and Amy in it? Why do you think Owen thinks this?
Overview	In what ways does the author create a sense of tension and suspense?

TALK FOR WRITING/DRAMA

If using the text with a group or as a class novel

- **Improvisation.** Imagine you are Amy Martin. Improvise a report which you are giving about the events of the first S.T.I.N.K. & Co. mission.
- **Hot seating.** Hot seat one or more of the characters at various points in the novel. For example, hot seat Mr Trovato after Mr Thorn has taken his ice cream van, Amy at the Trovatos' house as she awaits her parents, or Owen's dad after he has returned home with Owen.
- **Debate.** Is it right for S.T.I.N.K. & Co. to take action into their own hands and troubleshoot other people's problems?
- **Hypothetical happenings.** Discuss 'What ifs':
  - What if the story had been told from the point of view of Amy?
  - What if Mr Trovato hadn't believed Mr Thorn's story about why he was driving the ice cream van?
  - What if the tactics of S.T.I.N.K. & Co. had no effect on Shane Maxwell?
  - What if Owen had created O.I.N.K. & Co (otherwise known as Owen Investigates Nasty Kids Agency)?
  - What if…? (Create your own examples.)

RESPONSE TO THE TEXT

As ongoing work in reading journals

- Invent another agency. What acronym would you use? What would be your first mission?
- Create a portrait gallery of the agents in S.T.I.N.K. & Co. Label using information from the text.
- Imagine you are Stevie Trovato. Write a speech to brief your team on their next mission.
- Retell the story from the point of view of Stevie Trovato.
- Imagine you are one of the agents in S.T.I.N.K. & Co. Describe the events of your next mission.
- Summarise each chapter in no more than thirty words.

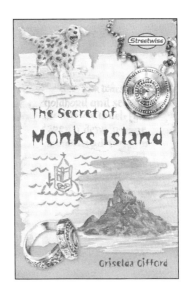

Synopsis:

Sam and her sister Alice are staying in a guest house run by Mrs Cuthbertson and her son, Eddie. Nearby, on an island, is a ruined church with a violent history. Sven, another guest in the house, claims to be researching that history, but in fact is seeking to steal the island's treasure. Eddie and Sam foil his plans.

TWENTY QUESTIONS

Chapter 1	What are your first impressions of Eddie Cuthbertson? What role do you think he will play in the adventure? Why?
Chapter 1	What are your first impressions of Sven? How do you think these compare with what Alice thinks of him at this stage? And with what Mrs Cuthbertson thinks of him?
Chapter 1	Consider the character of Bertie. Compare him with animal characters in other stories that you know. What do you think his role will be in the rest of the story? Why?
Chapter 2	From what we have learned in the first two chapters, compare and contrast the characters of Sam and Alice. What role do you think Alice will play in the rest of the story? Why?
Chapter 2	Do you think Sam is right to be suspicious of Sven? Why?
Chapter 3	How do your impressions of Eddie change during this chapter?
Chapter 3	At times, Sam has 'feelings' or imagines things happening. Why do you think this happens? Do you think the feelings are real?
Chapter 4	Consider Sam's father. How do you think he would react if he knew what Sam and Eddie know at this point in the story?
Chapter 4	Describe how Sven behaves with Mrs Cuthbertson towards the end of Chapter 4. Why do you think he does this?
Chapter 5	Why doesn't Alice seem interested in the medallion? Do you think she would show more interest if she knew the story behind it? Why?
Chapter 5	Loki the cat is named after a mischievous Viking God. In what other ways does Sam imagine that Loki is connected with the Vikings?
Chapter 6	Why does Eddie think that Sven being at the house at breakfast means that he has not found the treasure?
Chapter 7	Given what we already know about the relationship between Sam and Alice, why do you think Sam is so keen to rescue her sister?
Chapter 7	Why does Sven say to Mrs Cuthbertson, "or should it be *au revoir*?"?
Chapter 7	At the end of this chapter, the ancient book of the monks has gone. What are the implications of this?
Chapter 8	As Sam and Eddie approach the causeway, Sam imagines that she sees monks running along it, followed by Vikings. What do you think this signifies?
Chapter 8	When they open the tomb, Sam doesn't want Eddie to know how scared she is. Why not?
Chapter 8	What do you imagine Sven would have done if Bertie hadn't stopped him from coming down the steps?
Chapter 9	To begin with, the police don't seem to believe the story of Sam and Eddie. Why not? What happens to make them change their mind?
Overview	What devices does the author use to create suspense?

Novel Ideas

TALK FOR WRITING/DRAMA

If using the text with a group or as a class novel

- **Decision alley/thought tunnel.** At various points in the story, Sam and Eddie must make decisions. For example, should they follow Sven to Monks Island? Should they hand in the treasure trove or keep it secret? **Select a child to take on the role of either Sam or Eddie. Form two lines opposite each other to create the 'alley' or 'tunnel'.** As Sam or Eddie walks through the tunnel, take turns to offer advice on the course of action they should take. **Alternatively, make the two lines represent the two sides of Sven's conscience.** Each side of the alley states what Sven is thinking at any appropriate point in the story.
- **Role on the wall.** Sketch one of the characters from the story and surround with information about that character. For example, sketch Sven and surround him with facts derived from the text. **If dramatising the story, additional facts and information can be added during the drama, including the children's and other characters' opinions of him.**
- **Debate.** Should 'treasure trove' stay local and available to the public, or should it be sold to whoever can pay the most for it?
- **Hypothetical happenings.** Discuss 'What ifs':
  - What if Sam hadn't become friends with Eddie?
  - What if Sam's parents had insisted that Sam went with them to the hospital?
  - What if Alice had shown the medallion to Sven?
  - What if Sven Larsen had been able to swim?
  - What if…? (Create your own examples.)

RESPONSE TO THE TEXT

As ongoing work in reading journals

- Imagine you are Eddie. Keep a journal documenting events as they unfold in the story.
- Devise and label a map showing the location of the treasure on Monks Island. Indicate the position of the causeway, the guest house and other points of interest.
- Invent a police record for Sven Larsen.
- Design and write an invitation to Sam and Eddie inviting them to view an exhibition of the treasure at the local museum.
- Create the catalogue for the exhibition. What do the artefacts look like?
- Imagine you are an historian. Review the information given about Vikings in the text and create a fact file based on this.

TEXT FEATURES

In discussing adventure stories, some of the following textual features could be noted:

- Evident hero/heroine.
- Situations likely to concern games, playing, explorations, races, challenges, sports, travel, danger and risk-taking.
- Fast pace to storytelling.
- Strong focus on plot and action.
- Frequently concern a journey or element of discovery.
- Children's adventure stories generally concern adult-free groups.
- Plot structure often involves cliffhangers, especially at the end of chapters.
- Clear, dramatic climax; satisfactorily resolved at the end.

EXPLORATION OF THE GENRE

Key questions
- Can an adventure story also belong to another genre, e.g. fantasy adventure stories?
- What do we mean by 'an adventure'?
- Do you have to go somewhere else to have an adventure, or can it take place at home?
- Does an adventure always have to be exciting?
- Can adventure stories appeal to boys and girls equally?
- Which underlying themes work well in adventure stories? (e.g. environmental, social)
- What generalisations can you make about adventure stories?
- Have you read any other adventure stories? What kinds of adventure took place?

Possible activities
- Explore other adventure texts, e.g. 'choose your own adventure' stories, factual adventures.
- Create a checklist of things that children would need to take with them on an adventure. Make alternative lists, for example, cold adventures, river adventures, adventures in a back garden.
- Compile an ongoing class list of both fictional and factual adventurers (for example, Robinson Crusoe, Christopher Columbus). Tell the story of one of the adventures.
- Devise an 'adventure map', either from imagination or based on a story known to the children.
- Design activities or structures to be found in a 'fantasy adventure playground'.
- Make a list of any other adventure stories the class has read, with recommendations about who might enjoy them and why.

WIDER READING

- **The Wind Singer,** William Nicholson
Longman; ISBN: 058279661X
Kestrel hates exams and everything they stand for. But to say this in the city of Aramanth, where exams are eveything, is not wise, and when she does, her whole family are sentenced to the harshest punishment. Desperate to save them, Kestrel sets out on an adventure to discover the secret of the wind singer and the true source of the evil that grips Aramanth.

- **Adventure Stories (Story Library),** Clive King (Editor)
Kingfisher Books; ISBN: 0862728002
An anthology of adventure stories featuring work by authors such as Mark Twain, Jack London and Jan Needle.

- **Alice's Adventures in Wonderland / Through the Looking Glass,** Lewis Carroll
Penguin Classics; ISBN: 0141439769
When Alice follows a White Rabbit down a rabbit-hole, she little suspects the adventures that await her. A succession of weird and wonderful characters such as the Mad Hatter, Tweedledum and Tweedledee and Humpty Dumpty help and hinder her on her way home.

- **The Chronicles of Narnia,** C.S. Lewis
Collins; ISBN: 0007117302
A series of seven novels recounting the story of the magic kingdom of Narnia, domain of Aslan the lion, from its creation to a final battle. Children gain access to Narnia in a variety of magical ways, the best known of which is through the back of a wardrobe.

- **The Hobbit,** J.R.R. Tolkien
Collins Modern Classics; ISBN: 0006754023
A band of dwarves, under the leadership of Thorin Oakenshield, are on a quest to recover the gold which was stolen from them by Smaug the Dragon. They enlist the help of Bilbo Baggins, a peace-loving hobbit and unlikely adventurer. With the help of Gandalf the wizard, the dwarves and Bilbo cross the Misty Mountains and survive the perils of Mirkwood Forest. Reclaiming the gold from Smaug triggers a great battle, which claims the life of Thorin, but makes a hero of Bilbo, who is helped by his discovery along the way of a magic ring.

- **Journey to the River Sea,** Eva Ibbotson
Longman; ISBN: 0582795923
Maia, an orphan, receives news of some distant relatives, the Carters, who have agreed to look after her. They live in the Amazon rainforest and Maia is excited by thoughts of the new life that awaits her. However, on arrival, all is not as she had hoped. The Carters only agreed to look after her for money and have little affinity with their jungle home. Maia, on the other hand, likes life in the jungle, and in the end settles there after a series of adventures involving a travelling actor and a missing heir.

- **The Thief Lord,** Cornelia Funke
The Chicken House; ISBN: 1903434777
Two orphans, Prosper and Bo, run away together to Venice where they meet up with a gang of children and their leader Scipio, the Thief Lord. Hot on their trail is the private detective Victor Getz. Stealing to survive, the children agree to take on a job and steal a wooden wing, the missing part of a magical fairground ride, which has the ability to send the rider through time.

Genre-specific text features:

slapstick, characters' names reflect character traits, situation comedy, predictable plot, happy ending.

Key teaching objective:

Y5 T1 T3 To investigate how characters are presented, referring to the text:
- through action and description;
- how the reader responds to them.

INTRODUCTION AND STRATEGY CHECK

- Introduce the story by providing some background information about the text. 'Burglars' was originally one of a collection of short stories called 'The Incredible Adventures of Professor Branestawm'. Published in 1933, the stories were originally written for BBC radio but, due to their popularity, they were later sold in book form and then adapted for television in the 1960s. Has anyone heard of, or read any other books about Professor Branestawm?
- Ask one child to read aloud the first three paragraphs of the story.
  - What are your initial impressions of the Professor?
  - What technique does the author use to 'hook' the reader and introduce Professor Branestawm? (action)
  - How are we first introduced to Mrs Flittersnoop? (dialogue)
- Explain that another technique writers use to present characters is description. The author describes Mrs Flittersnoop's bonnet as '…the blue one with the imitation strawberries on it…'. What does this extra information tell the reader about Mrs Flittersnoop?
- Share the lesson objective with the group. Ask the children to divide a page in their reading journals and, when reading, to note down any words or phrases the author uses to portray Professor Branestawm and Mrs Flittersnoop. What do a character's actions tell us about them? What can we learn about a character by what is described?
- Recall/introduce a range of reading strategies and prompts appropriate to the group. What strategies can we use to help us read and understand an unfamiliar text?

INDEPENDENT READING

- Ask the children to read independently to page 9 ('She wondered where he could have got to.').
- Prompt individual children to interact with the text.
  - Why is the housekeeper called Mrs Flittersnoop?
  - On page 6, the author describes the 'special Professor lock'. What does this tell us about the Professor?

RETURNING TO THE TEXT AND RESPONSE

- Support discussion. Clarify points raised and review reading strategies.
- Discuss the character of Professor Branestawm. Ask the children, in pairs, to discuss what they have found out about him.
- Skim read back through the text. The Professor is portrayed as very absent-minded. What evidence can you find in the text to support this view?
- Discuss the character of Mrs Flittersnoop. How is she portrayed?
- Point out how the author uses other information to depict character. On page 5, the author describes what has been stolen. What extra information does this list give us?
- Discuss other characters. What can you infer about the character of Mrs Flittersnoop's sister Aggie?

FOLLOW-UP

- In preparation for Lesson 2, ask the children to continue reading to page 11 ('"Oh! He is a careless man to go losing himself like that!"').

Writing

- Ask the children to create a comic strip of the events in the story so far.
- Alternatively, ask them to imagine they are the Professor and to invent a new contraption. Draw a labelled diagram of the invention, with instructions.

Speaking and listening

- Form a 'Reading Circle'. Ask the children to review the text and identify how Norman Hunter creates the humorous character of Professor Branestawm. How would you create a female version of Professor Branestawm?

INTRODUCTION AND STRATEGY CHECK

- Introduce the story by providing some background information about the text. 'Burglars' was originally one of a collection of short stories called 'The Incredible Adventures of Professor Branestawm'. Published in 1933, the stories were originally written for BBC radio but, due to their popularity, they were later sold in book form and then adapted for television in the 1960s. Has anyone heard of, or read any other books about Professor Branestawm?
- Read aloud the first three paragraphs of the story.
    - What type of story are you about to read? How do you know? Who are the main characters? What do you notice about their names?
    - What technique does the author use to 'hook' the reader and introduce us to Professor Branestawm? (action)
    - Compare this with how the author first introduces Mrs Flittersnoop. (dialogue)
- Ask the children to skim read the first three paragraphs. What do we learn about the Professor by his actions? (absent-minded, always forgetting things, eccentric – the bell, boots on the wrong feet, uses five pairs of glasses, watches unusual films, invents things)
- Share the lesson objective with the group. Ask the children, when reading, to imagine the Professor and Mrs Flittersnoop. What do you think they look like? How do you know? How do they act? What do a character's actions tell us about them?
- Recall/introduce a range of reading strategies and prompts appropriate to the group. What strategies can we use to help us read and understand an unfamiliar text?

INDEPENDENT READING

- Ask the children to read independently to page 9 ('She wondered where he could have got to.').
- Prompt individual children to interact with the text. What is your impression of Professor Branestawm? What do you imagine the inventory is like? What do you think a mangle is? Are you enjoying the story? Why?

RETURNING TO THE TEXT AND RESPONSE

- Support discussion. Clarify points raised and review reading strategies.
- Discuss the character of Professor Branestawm.
    - Ask the children, in pairs, to discuss what they have found out about him.
    - On page 8, the author writes '…put on Mrs Flittersnoop's bonnet by mistake and went to the pictures again.' What does this action tell us about the Professor? Why is this funny?
- Discuss the character of Mrs Flittersnoop. How is she portrayed? How do you think the Professor views her? What evidence did you find to support your views?
- Anticipating events. Can you predict what has happened to the Professor?
- Personal response. If you had to choose the funniest moment in the story so far, which would you choose and why? Are you keen to read on? Why?

FOLLOW-UP

- Ask the children to continue reading to page 10 ('"Oh! He is a careless man to go losing himself like that!"').

Writing

- Ask the children to sketch and label the character of Professor Branestawm or Mrs Flittersnoop. Use evidence from the text to support your interpretation.
- Alternatively, in reading journals, draw a labelled diagram of the Professor's 'burglar catcher' and write a set of instructions explaining how it works.

Speaking and listening

- Form a 'Reading Circle'. Review the text and identify what it is about the characters that makes them funny.

Synopsis:
Professor Branestawm and his housekeeper go to the cinema and are shocked to discover on their return that their house has been burgled. The Professor decides to invent a 'burglar catcher', but ends up being caught by it himself when he forgets his keys one day.

Genre-specific text features:

slapstick, characters' names reflect character traits, situation comedy, predictable plot, happy ending.

Key teaching objectives:

Y5 T1 T10 To evaluate a book by referring to details and examples in the text.
Y5 T1 T12 To discuss the enduring appeal of established authors and 'classic' texts.

INTRODUCTION AND STRATEGY CHECK

- Recap Lesson 1 and clarify any points raised. Check that the children have read to page 11 ('"Oh! He is a careless man to go losing himself like that!"'). What do you predict has happened to Professor Branestawm? What evidence do you have to support your views?
- Refer back to page 3 ('"Mrs Flittersnoop," he said, looking at her through his near-sighted glasses...'). Ask the children to skim read the text to page 5 ('...and Mrs Flittersnoop went to bed.').
  - What clues can you find in the text to suggest that this story was written a long time ago? ('the Mickey Mouse one', 'latchkey', 'housekeeper', 'to give notice', 'picture-postcard album', 'best eggcups that were never used, except on Sundays')
  - Establish that these references illustrate differences in language use and ideas. What words might we use today instead of 'pictures' and 'latchkey'? What does the phrase '...best eggcups...Sundays' suggest about life at that time? (Sundays more formal, a 'special' day, best items saved for Sundays)
- Establish that 'Burglars' is regarded as a 'classic' children's story. What is meant by a 'classic' story? (high quality, lasting appeal, continues to be published, the character of Professor Branestawm is well-known)
- Share the lesson objectives with the group. Ask the children, when reading, to think about whether they would recommend this story to someone else and why. Would you consider 'Burglars' a classic story?

INDEPENDENT READING

- Ask the children to read independently to the end of the story.
- Prompt individual pupils to interact with the text. Under what circumstance would the Judge have imprisoned the Professor? In court, why did the Professor try on all of his pairs of spectacles 'one after the other'? What had the Judge done that was deemed 'dislegal'?

RETURNING TO THE TEXT AND RESPONSE

- Support discussion. Clarify points raised and review reading strategies.
- Discuss what makes 'Burglars' a classic. Having read the story, why do you think 'Burglars' is considered a 'classic'? Have you read any other 'classic' stories? Would you award 'Burglars' the title of classic children's story? Why?
- Written response.
  - Ask the children to 'star rate' the story. Use the following criteria: enjoyment and interest. Write a paragraph to justify the score.
  - Discuss responses.

FOLLOW-UP

Writing

- 'Ask the Publisher'. Imagine you are able to ask the publisher ten questions about the re-issue of the story. What would you ask?
- Alternatively, ask the children to imagine they are time travellers whose next destination is somewhere in the future hundreds of years from now. You decide to take along five children's books that you predict will be future classics. What would you take? For what reasons?

Speaking and listening

- Retelling the story. In pairs, retell the story onto audio cassette in the way it was originally planned to be, i.e. broadcast on the radio.

INTRODUCTION AND STRATEGY CHECK

- Recap Lesson 1 and clarify any points raised. Check that the children have read to page 10 ('"Oh! He is a careless man to go losing himself like that!"').
- Ask one child to summarise what happened after the Professor's burglar catcher went off. What do you predict has happened to Professor Branestawm? What evidence do you have to support your views? Has anyone found out any more information about the character of Professor Branestawm? Are you enjoying the story? Does the story live up to your expectations of a 'humorous' story?
- Establish that 'Burglars' is regarded as a 'classic' children's story. What is meant by a 'classic' story? (high quality, lasting appeal, continues to be published, the character of Professor Branestawm is well-known)
- Share the lesson objectives with the group. Ask the children, when reading, to think about whether they would recommend this story to someone else and why. Would you consider 'Burglars' a classic story?

Synopsis:
Professor Branestawm and his housekeeper go to the cinema and are shocked to discover on their return that their house has been burgled. The Professor decides to invent a 'burglar catcher', but ends up being caught by it himself when he forgets his keys one day.

INDEPENDENT READING

- Ask the children to read independently to the end of the story.
- Prompt individual pupils to interact with the text. What happened after the policeman 'undid the ropes and things' in court? What is funny about the court scene? How did the Professor end up getting caught in the 'burglar catcher'? Under what circumstance would the Judge have imprisoned the Professor? What did Mrs Flittersnoop do upon hearing that the Professor was to be set free?

RETURNING TO THE TEXT AND RESPONSE

- Support discussion. Clarify points raised and review reading strategies.
- Discuss what makes 'Burglars' a classic. Having read the story, why do you think 'Burglars' is considered a classic? Have you read any other classic stories? Would you award 'Burglars' the title of classic children's story? Why?
- Written response.
  - Skim read the text and list which parts you enjoyed/disliked, stating reasons. Use page references and quotations where appropriate.
  - Select several children to read aloud their responses.

FOLLOW-UP

Writing

- 'Ask the Author'. Imagine you are able to ask Norman Hunter ten questions about the story. From where did you get your inspiration? Did you model the Professor on someone you know? Did you base the story on your experiences?
- Alternatively, ask the children to imagine they are Mrs Flittersnoop. In reading journals, design and write a postcard to your sister Aggie informing her of recent events.

Speaking and listening

- Retelling the story. In pairs, retell the story onto audio cassette in the way it was originally planned to be, i.e. broadcast on the radio.

TALK FOR WRITING/DRAMA

Mantle of the expert

- Dramatise the story. Prior to the session, ask two children to become experts on inventing weird machines and to research similar crazy inventions, such as those drawn by Heath-Robinson. Using the technique of 'Mantle of the expert', the children present their findings to an audience at an appropriate point in the drama.

Debate

- Should Professor Branestawm be allowed to restrain a burglar until the police arrive?

Quote unquote

- Locate and discuss examples from the text which demonstrate:
  - that Professor Branestawm is eccentric
  - that Professor Branestawm likes inventing
  - that Mrs Flittersnoop is a busybody
  - that the court is a farce.

WRITING

- Professor Branestawm is advertising for an 'Assistant Inventor'. Write the advertisement detailing qualities required.
- Entries have been requested for the WIC (World Inventing Championships). Write a submission to the judges explaining why you think Professor Branestawm should win.
- The news of the Professor's trial soon hits the local headlines. Write a newspaper report to announce his release.
- Which part of the story did you find the funniest? Sketch the scene and use a quotation from the text as a caption.
- Write a further adventure for the Professor. What will he invent next?

AUTHOR OF 'BURGLARS' IN *BURGLARS, DUCKS AND KISSING FROGS*

Norman Hunter wrote the first Professor Branestawm stories for BBC radio. They were broadcast in the early 1930s. The first Professor Branestawm book, *The Incredible Adventures of Professor Branestawm*, was published in 1933. The story 'Burglars' comes from that book.

Norman Hunter was born in 1899 in London. He didn't enjoy school and when the First World War broke out in 1914 he volunteered to join the army. After the war he had three jobs: he learned to type and worked in advertising, he was a magician in the theatre, and he became a successful writer. He worked in South Africa for 20 years, then retired to live in London. He died in 1995.

This is how Norman Hunter described his life:

> I was born in London, 1899, a few years after the other Normans got there. After escaping from school I had a course in all-in wrestling with typewriters and eventually inserted my self into the advertising profession. I used to write advertisements of such allure that people bought vast quantities of the most unlikely things before they could stop themselves. I am also a conjuror, and managed to let off two hundred performances at Maskelyne and Devant's Theatre of Magic before the Nazis bombed my venue. By then I was in Bournemouth, but came back to London in time to be chased out again by flying bombs and finished the war living on a motor yacht on the Thames.

There are 16 books about Professor Branestawm, but some of them are out of print. The professor is an absent-minded inventor who wears five pairs of glasses at once (one pair to look for the others when he loses them!) His inventions include a paint-on carpet and machines for making pancakes, stroking cats and finding lost property. He is looked after by Mrs Flittersnoop, his sensible cook and housekeeper. His best friend is Colonel Dedshott of the Catapault Cavaliers, "a very brave gentleman who never missed a train, an enemy or an opportunity to get into trouble".

Norman Hunter's writing shows how he loved to play with words. In the book *Professor Branestawm's Dictionary*, the Professor invents his own definitions (for example, 'abominable – a piece of explosive swallowed by a male cow').

Other books by Norman Hunter you might also enjoy:
- *The Incredible Adventures of Professor Branestawm,* Puffin
- *Professor Branestawm's Treasure Hunt,* Puffin
- *The Peculiar Triumph of Professor Branestawm,* Red Fox
- *Professor Branestawm's Dictionary,* Puffin

Duck Boy   Jeremy Strong

Guided Reading   Lesson 1   Standard

Genre-specific text features:

comic situation, creating humour out of a serious event, slapstick, talking animals, happy ending.

Key teaching objectives:

Y5 T1 T3 To investigate how characters are presented, referring to the text:

- how the reader responds to them;
- through examining their relationships with other characters.

Y5 T1 T9 To develop an active attitude towards reading: seeking answers, anticipating events, empathising with characters and imagining events that are described.

INTRODUCTION AND STRATEGY CHECK

- Ask one child to read the first paragraph of the story. What do you notice about the opening of the story? In what ways does it capture the reader's attention?
- Ask another child to read the second paragraph of the story. Can you predict what might happen next? Why do you think this?
- Share the lesson objectives with the group. Ask the children, when reading, to focus on how the characters are portrayed. What is your impression of James' mother?
- Recall/introduce a range of reading strategies and prompts appropriate to the group. What strategies can we use to help us read and understand an unfamiliar text?

INDEPENDENT READING

- Ask the children to read independently to page 21 ('His nappy needed changing.').
- Prompt individual pupils to interact with the text. Focus on encouraging the children to adopt a more active approach to their reading. What makes this story funny? Which part have you enjoyed the most so far? What possible reasons does the author state for James' mother falling asleep? Does the predictability of the plot spoil the story for you?

RETURNING TO THE TEXT AND RESPONSE

- Support discussion. Clarify points raised and review reading strategies.
- Discuss the character of James' mother.
  - What is your impression of James' mother? Who is the victim in the story? To what degree would you say James' mother was irresponsible? Justify your answers with reference to the text.
  - So far, James' mother has spoken only once (page 20: "Where's my son?"), yet we already know quite a lot about her. What do we know?
- Discuss the minor character of the 'very untidy old lady'. Although we are not told much about her, what can we infer about her from her behaviour? (eccentric, without regard for the environment, quite strong)
- Discuss the role of coincidence in the story. Refer back to page 18 ('Now, by strange coincidence...kitchen.') and ask the children to skim read the first paragraph. How important is coincidence to the development of the plot? Does it contribute to the humour? What role do you predict coincidence will play in the rest of the story?
- Personal response. Which aspects of the story did you find funny? How does the author create humour?

FOLLOW-UP

- Ask the children to continue reading to page 25 ('Obviously it would not be long before people began to notice.').

Writing

- Ask the children to design a humorous leaflet outlining the potential perils of perambulators.
- Alternatively, tell them to imagine that they too were taking a walk beside the river that afternoon and saw the tragedy unfold before their eyes. In reading journals, write a witness statement describing the events as you saw them. Use sketches to support your account.

Speaking and listening

- In pairs, one child to assume the role of eye witness, the other the role of a police officer. Conduct an interview about the incident.

INTRODUCTION AND STRATEGY CHECK

- Read the first paragraph of the story to the children. What do you notice about the opening of the story? In what ways does it capture the reader's attention?
- Read the second paragraph to the children. Can you predict what might happen next? Why do you think this? What clues can we gain from the title?
- Share the lesson objectives with the group. Ask the children, when reading, to focus on how the characters are portrayed. What is your impression of James' mother? Who is the central character? How do you know? What do you know about the characters?
- Recall/introduce a range of reading strategies and prompts appropriate to the group. What strategies can we use to help us read and understand an unfamiliar text?

INDEPENDENT READING

- Read independently to page 20 ('His nappy needed changing.').
- Prompt individual pupils to interact with the text. How old is James? What possible reasons does the author give for James' mother falling asleep? How did James fall in the river? What makes this story funny? In your view, which part is the funniest? Why?

RETURNING TO THE TEXT AND RESPONSE

- Support discussion. Clarify points raised and review reading strategies.
- Discuss the character of James' mother.
  - What is your impression of James' mother? Justify your answer with reference to the text.
  - What do we know about James' mother from information in the text? What don't we know? (personal information – her name, etc., details about her life)
  - Hot seat James' mother. Jot down three questions each that you would like to ask her. The character responds in role.
- Personal response. What are your initial impressions of the story? Which aspects of the story did you find funny? Are you keen to read on? Why?

FOLLOW-UP

- Ask the children to continue reading to page 24 ('Obviously it would not be long before people began to notice.').

Writing

- In reading journals, write a set of rules that parents must follow when taking babies out in prams.
- Alternatively, design a 'Missing' poster offering a reward for information about the whereabouts of baby James.

Speaking and listening

- In pairs, one child to assume the role of James' mother, the other the role of a police officer. Conduct a telephone conversation between the two characters after the incident.

Synopsis:
When baby James' mother falls asleep, his pram rolls away down the hill and he falls into the river. Rescued by a family of ducks, James learns to live like them and even enters the 'Duck Olympics'. After several years, he is reunited with his mother.

Genre-specific text features:

comic situation, creating humour out of a serious event, slapstick, talking animals, happy ending.

Key teaching objectives:

Y5 T1 T2 To compare the structure of different stories, to discover how they differ in pace, build-up, sequence, complication and resolution.
Y5 T1 T10 To evaluate a book by referring to details and examples in the text.

INTRODUCTION AND STRATEGY CHECK

- Recap Lesson 1 and clarify any points raised. Check that the children have read to page 25 ('Obviously it would not be long before people began to notice.'). Were you surprised by what happened to James? How do you feel about what happened to him? What is your opinion about the style of humour used by the author?
- Ask the children to jot down in their reading journals the main events in the story so far. List them in chronological order.
- Establish that story structure varies between stories. Remind the children of the main stages in plot development (introduction, build-up, complication/conflict, resolution). Explain that short stories generally contain only one major conflict/complication and longer stories and novels may contain several. What is the 'conflict' in this story?
- Share the lesson objectives with the group. Ask the children, when reading, to think about the key events and overall structure of the story. How, and at what point, does the author introduce any new characters to the plot?
- Recall/introduce a range of reading strategies and prompts. What strategies can we use to help us read and understand an unfamiliar text?

INDEPENDENT READING

- Ask the children to read independently to the end of the story. Complete the list of the main events, using page references and quotations where appropriate.
- Prompt individual pupils to interact with the text. Why did the ducks find it very difficult at first to master front crawl? How did learning front crawl help other ducks and water birds? How did the ducks escape the hunters?

RETURNING TO THE TEXT AND RESPONSE

- Support discussion. Clarify points raised and review reading strategies.
- Ask one child to summarise the main events in the story. How was the conflict resolved?
- Demonstrate how to represent the story structure visually, e.g. sketch a line graph to represent the 'highs' and 'lows' of the story. Compare with a more complex novel that might have numerous complications. Have you read any stories with a similar plot structure?
- Discuss the mini 'parallel' plot, i.e. the very untidy old lady who 'flung' out her old washing-up bowl. Have you read any other stories that contain 'parallel' plots? Compare these with 'Duck Boy'.
- Personal response. What are your overall impressions of the story? Which part of the story did you enjoy the most? Why? Would you want to re-read the story? Would you recommend it to anyone else? Why?

FOLLOW-UP

Writing

- Ask the children to imagine they are James. In reading journals, write an autobiographical account of your life history from your earliest childhood memory to the present day.
- Alternatively, imagine they are a member of the camera crew from the television company Quacktion. Back in the cutting room, they need to decide which shots to include. Complete a storyboard of the key events in the story. Include quotations as captions.

Speaking and listening

- Years later, James swims at the Olympic Games. Ask the children to assume the role of sports commentator. Prepare and present an oral commentary on one or more of the swimming events in which James competed, for example, synchronised swimming, 200 metres front crawl and 800 metres individual medley. Include comments on style and technique.

INTRODUCTION AND STRATEGY CHECK

- Recap Lesson 1 and clarify any points raised. Check that the children have read to page 24 ('Obviously it would not be long before people began to notice.').
- Generate discussion about the text so far.
  - Were you surprised by what happened to James? In what ways did the family of ducks care for James? What did James teach the ducks? What did the family of ducks teach James to do?
  - On page 24, the author writes '…it was as if all the ducks had turned into mini powerboats.' What does this description suggest to the reader?
- As a group, discuss the main events in the story so far. Agree the chronological order of events and scribe the children's responses.
- Establish that story structure varies between stories. Remind the children of the main stages in plot development (introduction, build-up, complication/conflict and resolution). Where is the story set? What is the 'conflict' in this story? Explain that short stories generally contain only one major conflict/complication and longer stories and novels may contain several.
- Share the lesson objectives with the group. Ask the children, when reading, to think about the key events and overall structure of the story. How, and at what point, does the author introduce any new characters to the plot?
- Recall/introduce a range of reading strategies and prompts. What strategies can we use to help us read and understand an unfamiliar text?

INDEPENDENT READING

- Ask the children to read independently to the end of the story.
- Prompt individual pupils to interact with the text. How did the ducks think that James had saved their lives? For how long had James been missing? How did the newspapers and TV shows hear about the speeding ducks? Who named James 'Duck Boy'?

RETURNING TO THE TEXT AND RESPONSE

- Support discussion. Clarify points raised and review reading strategies.
- Ask the children in pairs to summarise the main events of the story. Complete the group list of main events.
  - Demonstrate how to represent the story structure visually, e.g. sketch a line graph to represent the 'highs' and 'lows' of the story. Compare it with a more complex novel that might have numerous complications.
  - On page 30, the author writes: 'Would James go back to land and live with his real mum, or would his real mum get into the river, learn to swim and be a duck? What do you think?' Discuss responses with reference to the text.
- Personal response. What are your overall impressions of the story? Which part of the story did you enjoy the most? Why? Would you want to re-read the story? Would you recommend it to anyone else? Why?

FOLLOW-UP

Writing

- Ask the children to imagine they are James. Create a timeline of events tracing your life story so far. Predict future events, giving reasons.
- Alternatively, create a fact file on James. Use the text to support your answer.

Speaking and listening

- 'A family of ducks heard James crying.' This event is the turning point in the story. In pairs, ask the children to discuss alternative scenarios. How else could James have been saved? In what ways would this have affected the outcome of the story?

Synopsis:
When baby James' mother falls asleep, his pram rolls away down the hill and he falls into the river. Rescued by a family of ducks, James learns to live like them and even enters the 'Duck Olympics'. After several years, he is reunited with his mother.

TALK FOR WRITING/DRAMA
Forum theatre
- Use the technique of 'forum theatre' to re-enact the scene when the hunters arrive to do some duck shooting. The audience assist the actors playing the characters by directing the action – dialogue, gestures, movement and so on. What might the hunters say when they see the ducks '…whooshing right past…whizzing up into the sky like rockets'? How might they behave? What might they think?
- A possible variation is to assign each child in turn the 'remote control', which he/she can use to pause, rewind, or fast-forward the action.

Debate
- Is James' mother to blame for losing her baby?

Hypothetical happenings
- Discuss 'What ifs'. Ask the children to create their own 'what if' examples.
  - What if the story began happily but ended in tragedy?
  - What if James' cries hadn't been heard by the family of ducks?
  - What if James had learned to fly?
  - What if the title of the story had been 'Zoo Boy'?
- Ask the children to create their own 'What if' examples.

WRITING
- Imagine you are James' mother. Write a diary entry for the fateful day your baby was lost.
- Imagine you are a writer for an online encyclopaedia. You need to redesign your 'FAQs' to include details about Duck Boy and his duck family. Write a set of FAQs and their corresponding answers.
- Imagine you are a newspaper journalist on the bank of the river. You are the first to witness James' mother arrive and you manage to get a scoop interview. In pairs, write and dramatise an interview between James' mother and the journalist.
- Write a bedtime story for young children in which Duck Boy meets one or more of the 'great duck heroes of the past – Donald, Jemima and Daffy'.
- Retell the story from the point of view of the ducks.

About the Author

AUTHOR OF 'DUCK BOY' IN *BURGLARS, DUCKS AND KISSING FROGS* AND *THE MONKEY'S TALE*

Ever since I was born, I have been surrounded by pets, mostly cats. But, I would have loved a monkey! Nearly all our pets have given us some kind of trouble. In particular I remember one of our cats, Ginger, coming through the cat flap with a whole roast chicken in his jaws! He'd swiped it from someone's kitchen windowsill!

I write in slightly different styles according to the kind of story I'm writing. *The Monkey's Tale* was a little more serious than 'Duck Boy'. You can't make the struggle for survival in winter into comedy! Generally I prefer comedy. I get fed up when everything is deadly serious. I want people to laugh most of the time.

I try my stories out on myself first by reading them out loud. It's a good way to get a feel for them. Sometimes I get one or two adults or children I know to read through and tell me what they think. Almost anything said about my work affects the way I think about my writing, and so it affects the way I actually write.

I often have no idea what I'm going to write next and that's scary. It's great when I have a firm idea about the next book – big sigh of relief! Like most writers I keep notebooks so if I get stuck for ideas I can leaf through the notebooks. Often I will find something that sparks off an idea and off I go again, writing away. I also talk to family and friends when I get stuck. Sometimes I ring another writer, Kaye Umansky, and talk to her. We phone each other up when we get stuck and we have a laugh over the phone and that helps too.

I mostly read animal stories and also a lot of non-fiction when I was young. The non-fiction was mostly historical science – how people did things long ago. I wanted to know how things worked. Nowadays I read all sorts, but mostly adult fiction and travel writers.

You can find a link to my website at www.storystreet.co.uk/streetwise/authors.

Awards
- *My Mum's Going to Explode,* was shortlisted for the 2002 Children's Book Award and won the Nottingham Big 3 Award.
- *Living with Vampires,* won the Short Novel 2001 Sheffield Children's Book Award.
- *Pirate Pandemonium,* won the Short Novel 1998 Sheffield Children's Book Award.
- *The Hundred Mile-an-hour Dog,* won the 1997 Children's Book Award.

Other books by Jeremy Strong you might also enjoy:
- *The Karate Princess and the Last Griffin,* Puffin
- *Krazy Kow Saves the World,* Puffin
- *My Dad's Got an Alligator!,* Puffin
- *There's a Pharaoh in Our Bath!,* Puffin
- *There's a Viking in My Bed!,* Puffin

Jeremy Strong also writes for the *Story Street* and *Info Trail* strands of *Literacy Land*.

Kissy, Kissy Louise Cooper

Guided Reading Lesson 1 Standard

Genre-specific text features:

parody of a well-known story, word-play, comic names and characterisation, reversal of expected situation.

Key teaching objective:

Y5 T1 T9 To develop an active attitude towards reading: seeking answers, anticipating events, empathising with characters and imagining events that are described.

INTRODUCTION AND STRATEGY CHECK

- Ask the children to look at the title and read the first two paragraphs of the story. What impressions do you have about the type of story you are about to read? Can you recall a humorous story that you have read before? What did you find funny about that? Why? What do you think is going to happen in this story? Give reasons for your answer.
- **Recall/introduce a range of reading strategies and prompts appropriate to the group.** What strategies can we use to help us read and understand an unfamiliar text?
- **Share the lesson objective with the group. Ask the children, when reading, to focus on empathising with the characters.** What does 'to empathise' mean? (to understand how someone feels and thinks) Contrast with 'to sympathise' (generally, 'to feel sorry for someone').

INDEPENDENT READING

- Ask the children to read independently to page 38 ('"…or I'm a frizzling fruit fly!"').
- Prompt individual children to interact with the text. Focus on supporting the children to adopt a more active approach to their reading.
  - What might become of Golp? What leads you to this conclusion?
  - On page 37, Grandma snorts "He ought to have his nobbles gurgled!" and "Not while I've still got blobs on my grummet!" What do you think she means? Why has the author chosen to use nonsense words? What does this tell us about the character of Grandma Glugga?
  - On page 36, the author uses brackets. Why?

RETURNING TO THE TEXT AND RESPONSE

- Support discussion. Clarify points raised and review reading strategies.
- **Discuss the character of Golp.** What is your impression of Golp? Do you sympathise with him? Why? Do you believe his story? How do the other characters react towards him?
- **Discuss the character of Gogglina.** What is your impression of Gogglina? Why did Gogglina first approach the prince? How do you think she felt? Justify your answers with reference to the text.
- **Personal response.** Which character do you empathise with the most? Why do you think the author chose the title 'Kissy, Kissy'? What alternative title could you choose? Why? Are you keen to read on? Why?
- **Hot seat one or more of the characters from the story.** Jot down three questions each that you would like to ask that particular character. The 'character' responds in role.

FOLLOW-UP

- In preparation for Lesson 2, ask the children to continue reading to page 41 ('"*Flies*," she said with relish.').

Writing

- In reading journals, ask the children to write a letter of advice to Golp or Gogglina explaining their views on the situation so far. Say what you would advise them to do next and why.
- Alternatively, assume the role of Golp or Gogglina. Write a diary entry for the day you met. What did you do? What are your hopes and fears?

Speaking and listening

- Ask the children to transform the story into a script. Assume the roles of the characters and dramatise the story so far. If possible, record on video.

INTRODUCTION AND STRATEGY CHECK

- Give the children the text and ask them to talk together in pairs for two minutes. What did you learn from the title? What impressions do you have about the type of story you are about to read? Can you predict what might happen in the story?
- Refer the children to the characters' names and highlight any tricky words. Recall/introduce a range of reading strategies and prompts appropriate to the group. What strategies can we use to help us read and understand an unfamiliar text?
- Give the children, in pairs, two minutes to read to page 33 ('"I'm a frog, just like you!"'). Prompt individual pupils to interact with the text.
  - Who are the main characters? How do you know?
  - What do we now know about the rest of the story? Does this story remind you of any other well-known children's stories?
  - What is your impression of Gogglina?
- Share the lesson objective with the group. Ask the children, when reading, to focus on empathising with Gogglina. What does 'to empathise' mean? (to understand how someone feels and thinks) Contrast with 'to sympathise' (generally, 'to feel sorry for someone').

Synopsis:
A handsome prince asks Gogglina the frog to kiss him, so that he can be turned back into a frog. First, the prince has to prove that he really was once a frog. Once turned back, he betrays Gogglina, whose grandmother resolves to get even.

INDEPENDENT READING

- Read independently to page 37 ('"Come on, my lad – it's test time."')
- Prompt individual children to interact with the text. Focus on supporting the children to adopt a more active approach to their reading.
  - On page 36, Grandma snorts "He ought to have his nobbles gurgled!" and on page 37, "Not while I've still got blobs on my grummet!" What do you think she means? Why has the author chosen to use nonsense words? What does this tell us about the character of Grandma Glugga?
  - Can you predict what will happen to Golp and Gogglina at the end of the story?

RETURNING TO THE TEXT AND RESPONSE

- Support discussion. Clarify points raised and review reading strategies.
- Discuss the character of Gogglina. What is your impression of Gogglina? Why did Gogglina first approach the prince? How do you think she felt?
- Discuss the character of Golp.
  - What is your impression of Golp? Refer to the text to support your answer.
  - If you were Golp, how would you feel to be 'human'?
  - Why do you think he is called Golp?
  - Golp hated being turned into a human. What would you hate being turned into?
  - What do you predict Golp's next test will be?
- Personal response. Are you keen to read on? Explain your reasons.
- Hot seat Grandma Glugga. Jot down two questions each that you would like to ask her. The character responds in role.

FOLLOW-UP

- In preparation for Lesson 2, ask the children to continue reading to page 39 ('"*Flies*," she said.').

Writing

- Ask the children to imagine they are one of the characters in the story. In reading journals, write a paragraph explaining your situation to a friend. Think about what has happened, and what is happening to them. How do you feel? What will you do next?
- Alternatively, write a character profile of one of the characters from the story.

Speaking and listening

- In pairs, one child to assume the role of a character from the story, the other the role of a news reporter. Conduct an interview for the radio station Croak FM. If possible, record on audio tape.

Genre-specific text features:

parody of a well-known story, word-play, comic names and characterisation, reversal of expected situation.

Key teaching objectives:

Y5 T1 T3 To investigate how characters are presented, referring to the text:
through dialogue.

Y5 T1 T13 To record their ideas, reflections and predictions about a book, e.g. through a reading log or journal.

INTRODUCTION AND STRATEGY CHECK

- Recap Lesson 1 and clarify any points raised. Check that the children have read to page 41 ('"Flies," she said with relish.').
- Ask one child to summarise the story so far. Can anyone predict what might happen in the rest of the story? What makes you think this?
- Refer back to page 35 ('"Wicked witch, pooey!" Grandma Glugga snorted.'). Ask the children to skim read the text to page 37 ('"…unless there's a reason as tasty as cabbage white butterflies!"'). What does this exchange tell the reader about Grandma Glugga? During the conversation, Gogglina hardly says anything and, when she does speak, she uses very short phrases. What does this tell the reader about Gogglina and her relationship with Grandma Glugga?
- Refer back to page 37 ('"Not while I've still got blobs on my grummet!"') and page 40 ('"Ponk me for a slug-sniggler…"'). How do these 'nonsense' expressions add to the characterisation of Grandma Glugga? Establish that the reader can learn a lot about a character by what they say and how they say it. Point out that 'Kissy, Kissy' is told mainly through dialogue.
- Share the lesson objectives with the group. Ask the children, when reading, to think about the characters. Who talks the most? Who talks the least? What can you learn about the characters by what they are saying?
- Ask the children to jot down in their reading journals any five examples of dialogue that the characters use which give the reader more information about them.
- Recall/introduce a range of reading strategies and prompts appropriate to the group. What strategies can we use to help us read and understand an unfamiliar text?

INDEPENDENT READING

- Ask the children to read independently to the end of the story.
- Prompt individual pupils to interact with the text.
  - On page 41, Grandma says "Stuff and newt-sense!" Why has the author chosen to include examples of word-play?
  - What does the exchange on pages 41–43 ('Bzzzz… "…and get on with it!" said Grandma.') tell us about the character of Golp?

RETURNING TO THE TEXT AND RESPONSE

- Support discussion. Clarify points raised and review reading strategies.
- Discuss the characters. On page 46, Golp says "Thanks, babe – I owe you one!" and "Get real, babe! Be seeing ya!" What does this tell the reader about Golp? Discuss examples noted.
- Explain that this type of story is sometimes called a parody (a literary work in which the style of an author or work is imitated for comic effect). What sort of story is it a parody of? Can you think of any other examples of parody?
- In pairs, ask the children to assume the roles of Golp and Grandma Glugga. Improvise a short conversation between the two characters.

FOLLOW-UP

Writing

- Description. Write a humorous paragraph to describe how you imagine Wily Wanda, the Well Wicked Witch.
- Alternatively, ask the children to imagine they are Golp or Gogglina's teacher. Write school reports for the two characters.

Speaking and listening

- Oral storytelling. In pairs, choose a well-known children's story to parody and tell the parody version to the rest of the group. If necessary, make brief notes as a reminder. Can the group guess which story you are parodying?

INTRODUCTION AND STRATEGY CHECK

- Recap Lesson 1 and clarify any points raised. Check that the children have read to page 39 ('"*Flies*," she said.').
- Ask the children to discuss in pairs what has happened in the story so far. Can anyone predict what might happen in the rest of the story? Why?
- Refer back to page 35 ('"Wicked witch, pooey!" Grandma Glugga snorted.'). Ask two children to assume the roles of Grandma Glugga and Gogglina and read out the conversation until '"…unless there's a good reason."' What does this exchange tell the reader about Grandma Glugga? What does '"…that story is a load of old snail slime"' tell us about the character of Grandma Glugga? Establish that the reader can learn a lot about a character by what they say and how they say it. Point out that 'Kissy, Kissy' is told mainly through dialogue.
- Share the lesson objectives with the group. Ask the children, when reading, to focus on thinking carefully about the character of Grandma Glugga. What can you learn about Grandma Glugga by what she says?
- Ask the children to jot down in their reading journals three examples of dialogue that Grandma Glugga uses which give the reader more information about her.
- Recall/introduce a range of reading strategies and prompts. What strategies can we use to help us read and understand an unfamiliar text?

Synopsis:
A handsome prince asks Gogglina the frog to kiss him, so that he can be turned back into a frog. First, the prince has to prove that he really was once a frog. Once turned back, he betrays Gogglina, whose grandmother resolves to get even.

INDEPENDENT READING

- Ask the children to read independently to page 47 ('"… Wait here!"').
- Prompt individual pupils to interact with the text. What does the exchange on pages 39–41 ('*Bzzzz…* … "…and get on with it!" said Grandma.') tell us about the character of Golp? What do we learn about Grandma Glugga? Look at what Golp says. What type of character do you think Golp is? Weak? Strong? Explain your answers.

RETURNING TO THE TEXT AND RESPONSE

- Support discussion. Clarify points raised and review reading strategies.
- Discuss the characters. What did you learn about Grandma Glugga? On page 45, Golp says "Thanks, babe – I owe you one!" and "Get real, babe! Be seeing ya!" What does this tell the reader about his character? What might Golp say if he was fond of Gogglina?
- Refer back to page 42 ('"Right," she said, when the Prince tottered back. "One last test."'). In pairs, ask the children to assume the roles of Golp and Grandma Glugga and read out their conversation in the ways that they would speak.
- Refer back to the text. On page 47, Grandma Glugga says "That gives me an idea. Wait here!" Can anyone predict what she has planned?
- Select a child to read to the end of the story.
- Personal response. Did you enjoy reading the story? Did you find the story humorous? Would you recommend it to anyone else? What was your favourite/least favourite part of the story? Are you satisfied with the end of the story? What might an alternative ending be?

FOLLOW-UP

Writing

- Ask the children to imagine they are out with friends and they overhear a conversation between Golp and Grandma Glugga. Write down their conversation. What might they say to each other and in what ways might they say it?
- Alternatively, create a Top Secret file on one of the characters. Include any information from the story and add any further information: likes, dislikes, date of birth, etc. Sketch a passport-sized photograph.

Speaking and listening

- In pairs, ask the children to take on the roles of Golp and Grandma Glugga. Improvise a short conversation between the two characters.

TALK FOR WRITING/DRAMA

Thought tracking

- Freeze-frame key incidents of the story and use the technique of thought tracking to reveal the character's thoughts at various points in the drama.
  - What might Gogglina have thought when she first saw Golp?
  - What might Grandma Glugga have been thinking when Gogglina first told her of Golp's request?
  - What might Grandma Glugga have been thinking when Golp managed to swallow twenty-three insects?
  - What might Golp have been thinking after he had finished singing his 'love' song to Gogglina?

Debate

- Did Golp's end justify his means? Did the fact that Golp so badly wanted to be a frog justify his treatment of Gogglina?

Fact or Opinion?

- Ask the children to use evidence from the text to decide whether the following statements are fact or opinion:
  - Golp likes to boast.
  - Golp doesn't like eating flies.
  - Grandma Glugga is a very kind frog.
  - Wily Wanda, the Well Wicked Witch, likes to help Grandma Glugga.
- Ask them to refer to the text and create their own facts and opinions.

WRITING

- Write a parody of another well-known children's story.
- Imagine you are a 'fly on the pond'. Write an eyewitness account of the main events in the story.
- Imagine you are a naturalist like David Attenborough. Write an encyclopaedia entry describing this particular breed of frog and its activities.
- Write a sequel to the story. Will Wily Wanda, the Well Wicked Witch, succeed in exacting revenge? Will Golp receive his 'just deserts'? What will become of Gogglina? Will she meet her 'Prince'?
- Write a review evaluating the story. Collate individual reviews and, as a group, create a composite review representing all views expressed. Make it available in the school library. Is the story a successful parody of 'The Frog Prince'?

About the Author

AUTHOR OF 'KISSY, KISSY' IN *BURGLARS, DUCKS AND KISSING FROGS* AND *BUTCH THE CAT-DOG*

I've always loved writing. When I was about 10, Mr Padgett, the Headmaster of my primary school, read out one of my ghost stories to the class. When he finished, he said, "Well, I don't know about anyone else, but it certainly scared me!" and I thought, "Yes! That's what I want to do for the rest of my life – tell stories!" Now, years later, and with more than 60 published books to my name, I'm still doing it.

I had terrific fun writing my two humorous *Streetwise* stories. 'Kissy, Kissy' was inspired by the traditional tale of 'The Frog Prince', but I gave the story a twist and added a new character – Grandma Glugga, who rules the Palace Pond and says ludicrous things like "Ponk me for a slug-sniggler!" (No, I don't know what she means, either!)

As for *Butch the Cat-Dog...* I absolutely love cats, and include them in a lot of my stories, so the chance to write a whole book about one was irresistible. I'm thankful to say that, except for his ginger colour, Tigger/Butch isn't based on any of my own cats! But I had a lot of catty help with the noises he makes!

If you've enjoyed my *Streetwise* tales, then you might also want to read *Sea Horses*, which is set on the Cornish coast, where I live, and tells the story of a broken statue, an ancient curse, and a strange white pony.

You can find a link to my website at www.storystreet.co.uk/streetwise/authors. You can get the news of my latest projects, and read "taster" chapters from my books.

Awards

* *Short and Scary!* is in the Red House Awards Top 100 for 2003.
* *Demon Crossing* was runner up in both the Angus Council Children's Book Awards 2002 and the Askews Torchlight Award 2002.

Other books by Louise Cooper you might also enjoy:
* *Sea Horses 1*, Puffin – (3 more to follow)
* *Short and Scary!*, Oxford University Press
* *Demon Crossing*, Hodder Children's
* *Hunter's Moon*, Hodder Children's
* *The Daughter of Storms trilogy*, Hodder Children's:
  * 1 - *Daughter of Storms*
  * 2 - *The Dark Caller*
  * 3 - *Keepers of Light*
* *The Mirror, Mirror series*, Hodder Children's:
  * 1 – *Breaking Through*
  * 2 – *Running Free*
  * 3 – *Testing Limits*

STYLES AND TECHNIQUES

Setting

In all three of the short stories, the settings are established in the first two paragraphs.

Writing

- In pairs, the children should skim read one of the stories and note down any words and phrases the author uses to describe a particular setting. Think about:
  - where the story is taking place. Using your senses, imagine what you can see, hear, smell.
  - over what period of time the story is happening. How do you know?
- Regroup the pairs and ask them to share findings. Are there any similarities about the settings? What are the differences?

Opening style

- In all three of the short stories, the main characters are introduced to the reader in the first two paragraphs. Re-read the first two paragraphs of each story. Ask the children to identify key features of the authors' styles. In what ways do the styles of the authors differ in the opening paragraphs?

Writing

- Ask the children to rewrite one of the stories in the style of another. For example, retell the story of 'Duck Boy' in the style of Norman Hunter (using slapstick humour or imbuing the characters with eccentric traits). Alternatively, retell 'Duck Boy' in the style of Louise Cooper (using dialogue and word-play).

Humour

- Ask the children to compare and contrast the authors' use of humour. Begin by focusing on the following three extracts (Standard Version page references):
  - 'Duck Boy', pages 21–22: 'They grabbed the washing-up bowl...like their own little ducklings.'
  - 'Kissy, Kissy', page 35–36: '"Wicked witch, pooey! ... he's got to prove it."'
  - 'Burglars', pages 5–6, 'Next morning the Professor was still inventing ... things of that sort.'
- Discuss what it is about each of these extracts that makes them funny. How is each author attempting to convey humour? Which devices do the authors use to create humour?
- Ask the children to find illustrative examples from other sections of the texts.

THEMES

Relationships

- In all three of the short stories relationships are very important. Ask the children to compare the ways in which the characters support each other.
  - Compare the roles of Mrs Flittersnoop and Grandma Glugga. In what ways are they similar?
  - Explain how Professor Branestawm, baby James and Gogglina are cared for. What are the similarities?
  - Who is the most dependent character? In your view, who is the most independent?

CHARACTERS

- Compare and contrast the major characters. For example, compare and contrast Mrs Flittersnoop ('Burglars') with James' mother ('Duck Boy') or Grandma Glugga ('Kissy, Kissy') with the Judge ('Burglars').

Writing

- Ask the children to create a comparison grid to compare and contrast key character traits and attributes.
- Compare the ways in which the characters are presented. Which characters would get on well? Which characters have similar personalities? Whom do you most admire? Why?

Debate

- Is Golp a villain? Is Professor Branestawm a hero?

CLASSIC VERSUS CONTEMPORARY

- Investigate the differences in language use across two of the texts. For example, 'Burglars' is told in a more formal, polite way and 'Duck Boy' in a more casual, anecdotal way.
  - How do you imagine the characteristics of the intended audiences for these stories have changed between the dates when 'Burglars' was published (1933) and when 'Duck Boy' was published (2003)?
  - What evidence can you find in the texts to demonstrate how people's attitudes have changed over time?

Writing

- Ask the children to find and list examples of pre-Second World War style language used in 'Burglars'. For example, 'housekeeper', 'latchkey', 'to give notice', and '… done some mending'.
- Ask the children to find and list examples of modern language used in 'Duck Boy'. For example, 'He chucked out teddy and rabbit', '… some very sloppy noises and filled his nappy' and 'the newspapers and TV shows got to hear about it'.
- Ask the children to write a contemporary version of 'Burglars'.

PERSONAL RESPONSE

- Ask the children to imagine the publisher has asked them to comment on each of these stories prior to publication. Write a letter in response, outlining your perception of the strengths of each story and areas for improvement. Refer to the texts to support your answers. Which of the stories is the funniest? Why? Which character did you find the funniest? Why?

Independent / Whole Class Reading

Synopsis:

Mikey and Edward want to enter the Dog Obedience Competition, but they only have a cat called Tigger and Tigger certainly isn't obedient. The only way to get Tigger to look and act like an obedient dog is to hypnotise him. Their plan is working well, until the hypnosis starts to wear off. In the end, the boys decide that a disobedient cat is better than an obedient dog.

TWENTY QUESTIONS

Chapter 1	From what we learn in this chapter, what can we say about the character of Tigger? What do we learn about him that has potential for creating humour later in the story?
Chapter 1	Having read the first chapter, how do you imagine the story might progress from here? What do you think might happen next, and why?
Chapter 2	Look at the way names are used in this chapter: for example, Butch, Tootsie and Yummy. How do these names create humour?
Chapter 2	Why do you think Tigger does not want to be trained? In what ways could the boys try to train him?
Chapter 3	Look at the text from the hypnotism book. Why are the words spelt in this way? What does this make us think about the book?
Chapter 3	Compare and contrast the way Tigger normally behaves with the way he behaves after the hypnotism. In what ways does this contrast create humour?
Chapter 3	Towards the end of this chapter, Tigger tries to bark. In what ways is humour used in this episode?
Chapter 3	Based on what you have read so far, how well do you think Tigger will do in the Dog Obedience Competition? Why?
Chapter 4	The two judges think that Tigger would be great in an advert for the latest horror film. What else could he advertise, either as Tigger or as Butch? Why?
Chapter 4	Describe how Tigger behaves in this chapter. In what ways would his behaviour have been different if he had not been hypnotised?
Chapter 5	In the opening section of this chapter, how confident do the two boys seem about Tigger's chances in the competition? Would you feel the same way, if you were them? Why?
Chapter 5	What do you imagine could go wrong when it is Tigger's turn in the competition?
Chapter 5	Describe the character of Esmerelda Pook. How is she used to create humour in the story?
Chapter 5	The performance of the mongrel is described as 'sort of okay. Ish.' What do you think this means? How else could it have been described? Why do you think the author chose to describe it in this way?
Chapter 6	Read how Tigger fares on the jump and seesaw. How is humour used here?
Chapter 6	Tigger's performance in the competition does not go as planned. How does it go wrong? Is this how you *expected* it to go wrong? Why?
Chapter 6	Based on what you have read so far, how do you think the story will end?
Chapter 7	Why do you think Edward prefers Tigger 'just the way he is'?
Overview	Which devices does the author use to create humour?
Overview	How successful is the novel in creating humour?

Novel Ideas

TALK FOR WRITING/DRAMA

If using the text with a group or as a class novel

- **Oral storytelling.** Retell the story around the group or the class, each child in turn adding two sentences.
- **Role on the wall.** Sketch one of the characters from the story and surround the sketch with information about that character. For example, sketch Butch, the 'Mongolian Orange Thingy', and surround him with facts derived from the text. **If dramatising the story, additional facts and information can be added during the drama, including the children's and other characters' opinions of him.**
- **Debate.** For a while, Butch makes a better pet than Tigger. Do cats or dogs make the best pets?
- **Hypothetical happenings.** Discuss 'What ifs':
  - What if Tigger had been a dog?
  - What if cats were allowed to enter the obedience competition?
  - What if Tigger had stayed hypnotised?
  - What if the 'Mongolian Orange Thingy' was really a type of dog?
  - What if …? (Create your own examples.)

RESPONSE TO THE TEXT

As ongoing work in reading journals

- Devise a 'Humour Graph', plotting levels of humour in each chapter.
- Imagine you own a copy of the book 'Howe to Hypno-Tyze Anythingge'. Write a paragraph to explain what you would hypnotise and why.
- Sketch a 'Barking Mad Amazonian Killer Crocodile' and explain how you would hypnotise it.
- Sketch and label one of the characters from the story. For example, sketch Miss Esmerelda Pook and her three dogs Tootsie, Petal and Honey-Bun.
- Rewrite Chapter 5 from the point of view of Miss Pook.
- Devise five questions you would like to ask the author, with reasons.

Independent / Whole Class Reading

Synopsis:

Prince Pantyhose is the spoilt son of King Wyfrunt and Queen Girdal. He lives a life of luxury, but longs to experience how the 'common people' of the kingdom live, and so swaps places with Jack, a humble faggot seller's son. He intends the swap to be temporary but it ends up being permanent.

TWENTY QUESTIONS

Chapter 1	The author begins the story with a classic fairy tale opening. Why do you think she does this? What does this tell you about the rest of the story?
Chapter 1	Describe what the text tells us about the Master of the King's Household. What can we infer about the way he would speak and act?
Chapter 1	What are your impressions of Cook? What can you infer about her?
Chapter 1	Look at the description of 'pottage'. What do you think pottage is? Describe how you think it would look, smell and taste.
Chapters 1 and 2	From reading the first two chapters, what are your impressions of castle life?
Chapters 1 and 2	How is the character of Queen Girdal portrayed?
Chapter 3	How does the Prince view his royal life, compared with the life of the common people?
Chapter 3	Compare and contrast the speech of Jack and the Prince. In your view, which words and phrases have been included to create humour?
Chapter 3	Do you think the Prince will enjoy life as a common person?
Chapter 4	Describe how you imagine the faggot seller's three daughters look.
Chapter 4	In what way do the faggot seller's daughters make fun of Prince Pantyhose? Why do you think they do this?
Chapter 4	Find examples of how the prince misunderstands the language used by this family of 'common people'. How does this contribute to the humour of the story?
Chapter 5	From what we see of him in this chapter, describe the character of the King. How does this fit in with what we already know about him?
Chapter 5	Describe the techniques Jack uses to make the King and Queen lower taxes. Why do you think they work?
Chapter 6	We hear that, as he grows older, the King spends more time on the 'royal privy'. Why do you think this is? Why is this funny?
Chapter 6	How do you think the real Prince Pantyhose would have gone down in history, if he hadn't changed places with Jack?
Overview	What devices does the author use to create humour? How successful are they?
Overview	Do the characters match your expectations of characters in this type of story?
Overview	What is the moral of the story?

TALK FOR WRITING/DRAMA

If using the text with a group or as a class novel

- **Freeze-frame.** Retell through drama one or more chapters of the story. Perform for an audience and freeze-frame key incidents: for example, when Prince Pantyhose swaps places with Jack, or when Jack passes himself off as Prince Pantyhose to King Wyfrunt. Record the still images on digital camera and capture onto presentation software such as PowerPoint to create an electronic storyboard. Use as a tool for organising writing.
- **Hot seating.** Hot seat one or more of the characters at various points in the novel. For example, hot seat Queen Girdal after Prince Pantyhose had left to mingle with the 'common herd'.
- **Debate.** Would Prince Pantyhose have lived a happier life if he hadn't swapped places with Jack?
- **Hypothetical happenings.** Discuss 'What ifs':
  - What if the Chief Cook had been good at cooking?
  - What if King Wyfrunt and Queen Girdal had realised that Jack wasn't the Prince?
  - What if Prince Pantyhose had been good at selling faggots?
  - What if Jack had come back to swap places with the Prince?
  - What if…? (Create your own examples.)

RESPONSE TO THE TEXT

As ongoing work in reading journals

- Devise a 'Humour Graph', plotting levels of humour in each chapter.
- Create titles for each of the six chapters. Give reasons for your choices.
- Consider the names of the faggot seller's three daughters: Ethelburga, Ethelbun and Ethelbred. Sketch and label them using information from the text to support your interpretation.
- Draw up a timeline of the main events in the novel.
- Imagine you are King Jack at the end of the story. Write a letter to Prince Pantyhose explaining why you did not return.
- Imagine you are a 'common person' in the market square and you see a familiar-looking faggot seller, who nonetheless does not seem to be very good at selling faggots. That evening, you are discussing the day's events with a friend. How would you describe what went on?

Independent / Whole Class Reading

Synopsis:

Olga finds a secret entrance in her garden which leads to a mysterious underground factory. In it she finds a pasty (or 'oggie') with magic powers. She goes on to find more oggies and she and her friend Sam enjoy using their magic powers, which allow them to stop time.

TWENTY QUESTIONS

Chapter 1	From what we learn in this chapter, what can we say about the character of Olga? What do we learn about her that has potential for creating humour later in the story?
Chapter 1	Describe what we find out about Olga's parents in this chapter. What role do you think they will play in the rest of the story?
Chapter 1	At the end of the chapter, Olga seems to find a secret entrance. Compare this with similar events in other stories that you know. How are they similar? How do they differ? Compare the situations in terms of the use of humour.
Chapter 2	Think back to when you were reading through this chapter for the first time. What did you think would be in the brown paper parcel? How did you feel when you found out it was an 'oggie'?
Chapter 2	At this stage, we have not yet found out what the magic power of the oggie is. What do you think it will be? Why?
Chapter 3	Describe the character of Uncle Billy and what happens to him in this chapter. What makes the episode humorous?
Chapter 3	Based on what we now know about the oggie's magic power, imagine other situations where Olga will be able to make use of it.
Chapter 4	Describe the character of Sam, based on what we learn in this chapter. What do we learn about him that has potential for creating humour later in the story?
Chapter 4	In this chapter, when Olga's father asks if she and Sam are having a treasure hunt, she replies 'Sort of'. Why is this answer appropriate?
Chapter 5	Describe the character of Mrs Harper. What is it about her that helps to create humour in the story?
Chapter 6	In this chapter, we see Olga being bullied. Bullying is not normally a humorous subject. How is it made to be funny?
Chapter 7	Read the second paragraph, and in particular the last sentence. What is funny about this? Why? What does it tell you about the character of Olga?
Chapter 7	Sam doesn't get to join in with eating the oggie in this chapter. Why do you think he doesn't mind?
Chapter 8	Describe the character of Walter. What is it about him that helps to create humour in the story?
Chapter 8	At the end of the chapter Miss Eagle reads to the class from 'Alice in Wonderland'. What connection does this have with events earlier in the story?
Chapter 9	Describe the character of Pixie. What is it about her that helps to create humour in the story?
Chapter 9	Describe what happens to Mr Reilly in this chapter. What is funny about this?
Overview	Review how Olga uses her magic oggies. Does she use them wisely? Why do you think this?
Overview	Which devices does the author use to create humour? How successful are they in this novel?

Novel Ideas

TALK FOR WRITING/DRAMA

If using the text with a group or as a class novel

- **Improvisation.** Improvise a further example of Olga using a magic oggie.
- **Decision alley/thought tunnel.** At various points in the story, Olga must make decisions. For example, should she tell Sam about the oggie? What should she and Sam do if they find another oggie? What should she do to stop Miss Eagle writing the questions for the science test? **Select a child to take on the role of Olga. Form two lines opposite each other to create the 'alley' or 'tunnel'.** As Olga walks through the tunnel, take turns to offer advice on the course of action she should take. **Alternatively, after each use of the oggie, make the two lines represent the two sides of Olga's conscience.** Each side of the alley gives opinions on how Olga has used the power of the oggie.
- **Debate.** Should Olga use the power of oggies only as a force for good, or should she use it for other purposes, such as to have fun, to take revenge, or to avoid having to obey rules?
- **Hypothetical happenings.** Discuss 'What ifs':
  - What if Olga had told her parents about the oggies?
  - What if Sam had stolen an oggie from Olga?
  - What if Walter ate an oggie?
  - What if the magic powers wore off halfway through an oggie?
  - What if…? (Create your own examples.)

RESPONSE TO THE TEXT

As ongoing work in reading journals

- Devise a 'Humour Graph', plotting levels of humour in each chapter.
- Sketch and label the underground 'factory', using information from the text to support your interpretation.
- Imagine finding a magical object wrapped in brown paper. Write a riddle/rhyme to explain what the finder must do and what magic lies in store.
- Write a newspaper report with the headline 'Fearless Plymouth schoolgirl discovers secret plans for Tamar Tunnel'.
- Imagine you are Sam. Keep a diary of events as the story unfolds.
- Write a paragraph explaining what you would do if you possessed a 'magic time-stopping oggie'.

TEXT FEATURES

In discussing humorous stories, some of the following textual features could be noted:

- Language play: puns, rhyme, jokes, riddles, double entendres.
- Use of nonsense words.
- Rhyme, alliteration or assonance to create comic effect.
- Predictable plot that allows for anticipation of joke. Plot often secondary to humour.
- Endings generally 'happy'.
- Omniscient narrator: provides asides, comments on action.
- Story told in an informal, anecdotal way.
- Presentational devices: different typefaces, italics, bold, capitalisation, design features.
- Characters possess a peculiarity of some kind – unusual idiosyncrasies of behaviour, mannerisms, appearance, speech.
- Plot structure often picaresque – roguish characters with multiple adventures.
- Characters' names frequently descriptive of character traits.
- Situation – what's happening is intrinsically funny in that it overturns the normal order of things. Characters in absurd situations, performing absurd tasks.

EXPLORATION OF THE GENRE

Key questions
- What makes you laugh in books or films?
- What do we mean by a 'sense of humour'?
- What devices do authors use to create humour?
- What would you expect to find on the cover of a humorous text?
- Imagine you are the main character in a humorous story. In what ways would you like to be funny?
- Can a television programme or film be called a comedy if it doesn't make you laugh?
- What generalisations can you make about humorous stories?
- Have you read any other humorous stories? How was humour created in those?

Possible activities
- Create a class 'Joke Box'.
- Design a recipe for a humorous story. What are the main ingredients? In what proportions would you include them?
- Explore inappropriate forms of humour. Discuss what is and isn't appropriate to laugh at.
- Describe how we can be humorous without using spoken or written language (e.g. gesture, facial expression, etc.). How can this be used to support language-based humour?
- Explore other types of humorous texts, e.g. comics, joke books, humorous poetry. Add your own examples.
- Collect further examples of words/phrases and narrative devices used to create humour while reading all types of humorous texts, including adverts.
- Make a list of any other humorous stories the class has read, with recommendations about who might enjoy them and why.

WIDER READING

- **Artemis Fowl,** Eoin Colfer
  Puffin Books; ISBN: 0141312122
  Artemis Fowl is a twelve-year-old criminal mastermind. His latest money-making scheme is to steal the legendary gold of the fairies, and to this end he kidnaps Captain Holly Short of the LEPrecon unit. However, these fairies are not prepared to let their gold go lightly, and come after him armed with heavy weapons and a lethal troll.

- **"The Fib" and Other Stories,** George Layton
  Macmillan Children's Books; ISBN: 0330397958
  A collection of funny and moving short stories, about life growing up in the 1950s.

- **The Frog Princess,** E.D. Baker
  Bloomsbury Children's Books; ISBN: 0747560749
  A parody of the traditional tale 'The Frog Prince'. Princess Esmerelda kisses an enchanted frog who claims he is Prince Eadric but, instead of turning into a prince, the princess turns into a frog. Together the two frogs seek the witch who cast the original spell on Eadric, but find themselves captured by an aspiring witch Vannabe. After various trials and tribulations, the spell is lifted.

- **Madame Doubtfire,** Anne Fine
  Longman; ISBN: 0582292611
  There's something strange about Miranda Hilliard's new cleaner-come-childminder, but Miranda can't quite work out what it is. Still, the children adore her, the house is spotless so what could possibly go wrong?
  Madame Doubtfire has been made into a fim starring Robin Williams and was retitled Mrs Doubtfire.

- **The New Cut Gang: Thunderbolt's Waxwork,** Philip Pullman
  Puffin Books; ISBN: 0140364102
  Thunderbolt Dobney is part of the 'New Cut Gang', who roam the streets of Lambeth. In this tale, they are looking for the source of forged coins that keep coming into circulation. For a while, it seems Thunderbolt's dad, an inventor, might be the culprit. However, the gang proves his innocence by using a madcap plan based on a waxwork dummy.

- **The Phantom Tollbooth,** Norton Juster
  Collins Modern Classics; ISBN: 0006754252
  Bored and fed up, Milo comes home from school one day to find an enormous package awaiting him – a 'genuine turnpike tollbooth'. He sets off through the tollbooth on a pun-ridden journey. He passes through the cities of Dictionopolis and Digitopolis, and meets characters including the Whether Man, King AZIZ the Unabridged and, most importantly, the princesses Rhyme and Reason.

- **The Twits,** Roald Dahl
  Puffin Books; ISBN: 014131138X
  The two revolting characters Mr and Mrs Twit spend much of their time playing tricks on each other. When not doing this, they are coating trees in glue in order to catch birds to make into Bird Pie, or tormenting their group of captive monkeys. The birds and monkeys exact revenge with some judicious use of the glue.

Genre-specific text features:

animals are characterised, readers are encouraged to sympathise and be respectful towards certain types of animals, main character is an animal.

Key teaching objectives:

Y5 T3 T1 To investigate a range of texts from different cultures, considering patterns of relationships, social customs, attitudes and beliefs:

- identify these features by reference to the text;
- consider and evaluate these features in relation to their own experience.

Y5 T3 T8 To record predictions, questions, reflections while reading, e.g. through the use of a reading journal.

INTRODUCTION AND STRATEGY CHECK

- Introduce the story by providing some background information about the text. First published in 1894, the story forms part of Rudyard Kipling's 'The Jungle Book'. 'Jungle Book', the Disney musical animation with characters such as Mowgli and Shere Khan, was loosely based on Kipling's works. Has anyone seen the film or heard of these characters? There are two 'Jungle Books': 'The Jungle Book' and 'The Second Jungle Book', which contain many stories; the best known are the Mowgli stories in which Mowgli the 'man-cub' is raised by wolves.
- Ask the children to read the first two paragraphs of the story. Where do you think the story might be set? How do you know? Establish that the story is set in the jungles of central India towards the end of the nineteenth century. Point out that 'Segowlee cantonment' is a military camp and that, in Gujarati, 'darzee' means tailor.
- Share the lesson objectives with the group. Ask the children, when reading, to think about the setting for the story. In reading journals, they should jot down any words or phrases used which indicate the setting for the story and any aspects of culture described. How does the way of life described differ from your own?
- Recall/introduce a range of reading strategies and prompts appropriate to the group. What strategies can we use to help us read and understand an unfamiliar text?

INDEPENDENT READING

- Read independently to page 9 ('"Look, and be afraid!"').
- Prompt individual children to interact with the text. Point out that 'nag' means snake in Gujarati. Who is 'the great god Brahm'? (supreme Hindu god)

RETURNING TO THE TEXT AND RESPONSE

- Support discussion. Clarify points raised and review reading strategies.
- Discuss the setting of the story. What evidence did you find that the story is set in an Indian jungle? What is a 'bungalow'? Explain that the word 'bungalow' has been borrowed from Gujarati.
- Discuss aspects of culture. What aspects of culture are described? (e.g. pages 5–6, 'verandah', 'bath tubs', 'ink on a writing table') From this information, what can you deduce about life at this time for the 'Englishman'? Does their way of life differ from your way of life? In what ways is it similar?
- Written response: 'Ask a Character'. Based on what you have read so far, write five questions to put to Teddy's father.

FOLLOW-UP

- In preparation for Lesson 2, ask the children to continue reading to page 12 ('But he is so small … more harm to people.').

Writing

- Ask the children to write a prediction for how the story will unfold.
- Alternatively, imagine you are Teddy's mother. Write a diary entry describing events on the day of Rikki-tikki's arrival.

Speaking and listening

- Form a 'Reading Circle'. Ask the children to review the text and identify how Kipling portrays Rikki-tikki-tavi. How does the reader respond to him? Why do you think he appeals to children?

Synopsis:
Washed away by a high summer flood, Rikki-tikki-tavi, the mongoose, finds himself in the care of Teddy's family. When hunting in their garden, he meets Darzee, the tailor-bird, and his family. Darzee is worried that the snake Nag will eat his babies. Rikki-tikki helps to save Darzee's babies, and also Teddy's family, from the menace of the snake.

INTRODUCTION AND STRATEGY CHECK

- Introduce the story by providing some background information about the text. First published in 1894, the story forms part of Rudyard Kipling's 'The Jungle Book'. Has anyone heard of 'The Jungle Book'? Point out that the popular Disney animation 'Jungle Book', with characters such as Mowgli, Baloo and Shere Khan, was loosely based on Kipling's works. Has anyone seen the film or heard of these characters? There are two 'Jungle Books': 'The Jungle Book' and 'The Second Jungle Book', which contain many stories; the best known are the Mowgli stories in which Mowgli the man-cub is raised by wolves.
- Read aloud the first two paragraphs of the story. What have you noticed about the story? Where do you think the story might be set? How do you know? **Establish that the story is set in the jungles of central India towards the end of the nineteenth century.** Highlight that, in Gujarati, 'darzee' means tailor.
- Share the lesson objective with the group. Ask the children, when reading, to think about the way of life presented in the story. How is the way of life described? How does the way of life described differ from your own?
- Recall/introduce a range of reading strategies and prompts appropriate to the group. What strategies can we use to help us read and understand an unfamiliar text?

INDEPENDENT READING

- Ask the children to read independently to page 8 ('"Look, and be afraid!"').
- Prompt individual children to interact with the text. What is the motto of all the mongoose family? What does it mean? In what ways is Rikki-tikki a 'true mongoose'? How did Rikki-tikki first make friends with Teddy? What name is Teddy short for? What is a 'bloodhound'? What is the 'spread hood' of Nag?

RETURNING TO THE TEXT AND RESPONSE

- Support discussion. Clarify points raised and review reading strategies.
- In pairs, ask the children to summarise the story so far.
- Discuss the way of life described in the story.
  - Refer back to page 3. What is a 'bungalow'? **Explain that the word 'bungalow' has been borrowed from Gujarati.** Does anyone here live in a bungalow?
  - Refer to page 6 ('He spent all that day roaming over the house.'). What words and phrases can you find which indicate how Teddy and his family live? (page 6, 'bath tubs', 'ink on a writing table', 'big man's cigar', 'Teddy's nursery', 'lamps were lighted', 'If a snake came ...') What is your impression of their way of life? Does their way of life differ from your way of life? In what ways is it similar?
- Written response. Ask a character. Based on what you have read so far, write three questions to Teddy and his family about their way of life.
- Personal response. What do you predict will happen in the rest of the story? What makes you think this? Are you keen to read on? Explain your reasons.

FOLLOW-UP

- In preparation for Lesson 2, ask the children to continue reading to the end of page 10 ('But he is so small ... more harm to people.').

Writing

- Suggest the children research information about mongooses. Sketch and label Rikki-tikki based on this information and information from the text.
- Alternatively, summarise the story so far in ten sentences.

Speaking and listening

- Form a Reading Circle. Rikki-tikki or Nag? Discuss which animal you would rather have as a pet and why.

Genre-specific text features:

animals are characterised, readers are encouraged to sympathise and be respectful towards certain types of animals, main character is an animal.

Key teaching objectives:

Y5 T3 T8 To record predictions, questions, reflections while reading, e.g. through the use of a reading journal.

Y5 T3 T10 To write discursively about a novel or a story, e.g. to describe, explain, or comment on it.

INTRODUCTION AND STRATEGY CHECK

- Recap Lesson 1 and clarify any points raised. Check that the children have read to page 12 ('But he is so small...harm to people.').
- Analyse the text. On page 9, the author describes Nag's 'hood' as having 'the spectacle-mark...hook-and-eye fastening.' What do you think he means? What do you think Rikki-tikki will do next? Why?
- Share the lesson objectives with the group. Ask the children to imagine they are literary critics; their job is to analyse and judge works of literature. With this in mind, ask the children, when reading, to make very brief notes in their reading journals of any points they wish to make about the text (e.g. views on the characters, part they most enjoyed, whether worth reading, words or phrases that are particularly descriptive or striking). Use quotations and page references if appropriate. What are your views on the characters? Do you think Kipling portrays them well? Are there any words or phrases that you feel deserve a mention?
- Recall/introduce a range of reading strategies and prompts appropriate to the group. What strategies can we use to help us read and understand an unfamiliar text?

INDEPENDENT READING

- Ask the children to read independently to the end of the story.
- Prompt individual children to interact with the text. For what reason did Rikki-tikki keep himself thin? Why was fighting Karait more dangerous than fighting Nag? Why do Nag and Nagaina want to kill both Rikki-tikki and the people? What is meant by 'one second's purchase' (page17)?

RETURNING TO THE TEXT AND RESPONSE

- Support discussion. Clarify points raised and review reading strategies.
- Review work completed in reading journals. In your role as 'literary critic', what are your overall impressions of the story? What are your views on the characters? Did you note down any words or phrases you felt deserved a mention? Why? Are there any aspects of the story you would change? Why?
- Written and oral response. Ask the children to list five positive aspects about the story which they feel would encourage someone else to read it. Discuss the list with a partner, who can challenge these views if they wish.

FOLLOW-UP

Writing

- Ask the children to imagine they are a literary critic. Write a review of the story for a broadsheet newspaper. You may wish to comment on the characters, aspects of vocabulary, plot and the ending.
- Alternatively, write a poem retelling events in the story.

Speaking and listening

- In groups, ask the children to imagine they are a team of aspiring film-makers (scriptwriters, wardrobe, special effects and producers), who wish to produce a film version of 'Rikki-Tikki-Tavi'. Prepare a presentation of your ideas for potential investors; include a script and a storyboard for a key scene in the film, details of special effects and wardrobe. Present to another group or to the class with the aim of securing funding so that your film can be made.

INTRODUCTION AND STRATEGY CHECK

- Recap Lesson 1 and clarify any points raised. Check that the children have read to the end of page 10 ('But he is so small...harm to people.').
- **Analyse the text.** Why was Nag secretly afraid of Rikki-tikki? How did Nag attempt to catch Rikki-tikki off his guard? What do you think Rikki-tikki will do next? Why? Why does Karait do more harm to people than Nag?
- Share the lesson objectives with the group. Ask the children, when reading, to reflect on the text and make very brief notes in their reading journals of any points they wish to make. What do you think of Rikki-tikki-tavi? Which part did you most enjoy? Why? Would you recommend the story to anyone else? Why?
- Recall/introduce a range of reading strategies and prompts appropriate to the group. What strategies can we use to help us read and understand an unfamiliar text?

INDEPENDENT READING

- Ask the children to read independently to the end of the story.
- Prompt individual children to interact with the text. Why do Rikki-tikki's eyes sometimes grow red? How did Rikki-tikki manage to kill Karait? Why do you think Teddy's father beat the dead Karait with his stick? Why do Nag and Nagaina want to kill both Rikki-tikki and the people?

RETURNING TO THE TEXT AND RESPONSE

- Support discussion. Clarify points raised and review reading strategies.
- In pairs, ask the children to briefly summarise the story.
- Review work completed in reading journals. What are your overall impressions of the story? Which part did you enjoy the most? Why? What are your views on the characters? Which character do you most admire? Why? Would you recommend the story? Why?
- Written response.
  - Ask the children to imagine they have already written a review of the story. The publisher wishes to include on the cover of the book a quotation from their review. Write a positive comment of the story in one or two sentences. Include name and age.
  - Ask the children to read out the comments and vote for the one which most accurately captures the story.

FOLLOW-UP

Writing

- Ask the children to imagine they are a designer working for a book publisher. Design an A4 sized advertisement for the book 'Rikki-Tikki-Tavi' to be displayed in libraries nationally.
- Alternatively, write an alternative blurb for the story.

Speaking and listening

- In pairs, ask the children to imagine they have been asked to produce a film version of 'Rikki-Tikki-Tavi'. Prepare a presentation of your ideas; include a script and a storyboard for a key scene in the film, details of special effects and wardrobe. Present to another pair or to the whole class.

Synopsis:
Washed away by a high summer flood, Rikki-tikki-tavi, the mongoose, finds himself in the care of Teddy's family. When hunting in their garden, he meets Darzee, the tailor-bird, and his family. Darzee is worried that the snake Nag will eat his babies. Rikki-tikki helps to save Darzee's babies and also Teddy's family, from the menace of the snake.

TALK FOR WRITING/DRAMA

Improvisation

- In pairs, one to assume the role of Teddy's mother Alice, the other the role of an interviewer. Conduct an interview to discuss how Alice's opinions of Rikki-tikki have changed in the course of the story.

Debate

- Teddy's father shoots Nag. Do humans have the right to kill wild animals in their garden?

Fact or opinion?

- Ask the children to use evidence from the text to decide whether the following statements are 'fact' or 'opinion':
  - The motto of all the mongoose family is 'Run and find out'.
  - Rikki-tikki is a true mongoose.
  - Teddy is seven years old.
  - Teddy's mother is frightened of Rikki-tikki.
  - Nag is feared by all in the jungle.
- Ask them to refer to the text and create their own facts and opinions.

WRITING

- 'This is the story of the great war that Rikki-tikki-tavi fought single-handed, through the bath-rooms of the big bungalow in Segowlee.' What other battles has Rikki-tikki fought? Write a short story to recount another of his battles.
- Retell the story from the point of view of Nag.
- Imagine you are a jungle explorer. Write entries in your log book to describe your observations of Rikki-tikki and Darzee and his family.
- Research Rudyard Kipling and write a mini biography.
- Which part of the story did you find the most exciting? Create a storyboard of the scene to show how the action develops.

About the Author

AUTHOR OF 'RIKKI-TIKKI-TAVI' IN *THE ELEPHANT, THE HARE AND THE BLACK COBRA*

'Rikki-Tikki-Tavi' is a story from *The Jungle Book*, written by Rudyard Kipling in 1894. There are two Jungle Books (*The Second Jungle Book* came out in 1895), both set in India; they tell stories of the jungle animals and a boy called Mowgli, 'the mancub'.

Rudyard Kipling loved India. His parents were English people who were living in Bombay when Rudyard was born in 1865. (They named Rudyard after a lake in Staffordshire where they had met.) Kipling's early years in India, living with his parents and his younger sister, Alice, were very happy.

When he was six, Rudyard and Alice Kipling were sent to live with foster parents in England. They were very unhappy; Kipling called their foster home 'the House of Desolation'. At the age of 12, Rudyard was sent away to a boarding school in Devon. He later wrote a famous school story, called *Stalky and Co.*, based on his experiences there.

When he left school in 1882, Kipling returned to India and started work as a journalist on a daily newspaper. He also wrote poems and stories which were published first in the newspapers and later as books. His work was very successful in India and by the late 1880s it had also become very popular in England.

Kipling married an American and had three children, Josephine, Elsie and John. Josephine died at the age of six; John died as a soldier at the the age of eighteen in the First World War. Kipling lived until 1936. He is buried in Westminster Abbey, in Poet's Corner.

If you enjoyed 'Rikki-Tikki-Tavi' you might like to read more of *The Jungle Books* or the *Just So Stories*, Kipling's fables about animals.

The Jungle Book has been made into a Disney film and there are lots of retellings of Kipling's stories in print.

Awards
- Kipling was offered many honours and prizes for his work, and he accepted the Nobel Prize for Literature in 1907.

Other books by Rudyard Kipling you might also enjoy:
- *The Jungle Book,* Penguin Popular Classics
- *The Second Jungle Book,* Puffin Classics
- *Just So Stories,* Penguin Popular Classics

Genre-specific text features:

animals are characterised; animals are standard characters in fables; theme of animal survival and freedom; main character is an animal.

Key teaching objective:

Y5 T3 T8 To record predictions, questions, reflections while reading, e.g. through the use of a reading journal.

INTRODUCTION AND STRATEGY CHECK

- Ask one child to read the first paragraph of the story. Who is telling the story? How do you know? (e.g. page 19, 'Why don't *we* have them?') How does the introduction serve to 'hook' the reader? What type of story do you predict you are about to read? (fable) Why? (anticipation of explanation, animals)
- Recall/introduce a range of reading strategies and prompts appropriate to the group. What strategies can we use to help us read and understand an unfamiliar text?
- Share the lesson objective with the group. Ask the children, when reading, to record their predictions for the rest of the story and to say why.

INDEPENDENT READING

- Ask the children to read independently to page 22 ('You'd have thought they owned the river.').
- Prompt individual children to interact with the text. The elephants have names like Mango and Wallow – why do you think the author chose this type of name? Why did elephants once have 'soft skin'? On pages 20–23, the author uses brackets. Why?
- Review predictions. What do you think will happen next? Why? Have you noted down any quotations to support your predictions? (e.g. page 21, '… when they had to leave the water …'; 'The elephants would have stayed in their underwater world forever')
- Ask the children to continue to read independently to the middle of page 25 ('And what she saw was Sneaker.'), continuing to note their predictions.
- Review predictions again. What do you think will happen next? Have you noted down any quotations to support your predictions? (e.g. page 23, 'Games were … just wasn't fair!'; page 24, 'Soon, Mango … *Two* chances.')

RETURNING TO THE TEXT AND RESPONSE

- Support discussion. Clarify points raised and review reading strategies. Did anyone manage to jot down any questions to the author?
- Analyse the characters of Mango and Sneaker. Divide a page in your reading journals. In pairs, skim read back through the text and note down what can be inferred about the two characters.
- Personal response. Are you keen to read on? Explain your reasons.

FOLLOW-UP

- In preparation for Lesson 2, ask the children to continue reading to page 29 ('"Come on," she whispered…"Let's explore."') and jot down in their reading journals their amended predictions for the rest of the story and why.

Writing

- Ask a Character. In reading journals, compose ten questions you would like to ask one of the characters from the story.
- Alternatively, ask the children to assume the roles of 'Agony Aunt' or 'Agony Uncle' and Mango. Write an exchange of letters between the two characters.

Speaking and listening

- Ask the children to think of a natural phenomenon such as why stars twinkle. In pairs, make up a story in the style of 'The Underwater Elephants' to explain the phenomenon, and present to the rest of the group or to the class.

INTRODUCTION AND STRATEGY CHECK

- Read the first paragraph of the story. What do you notice about the beginning of the story? Who is telling the story? How do you know? (e.g 'Why don't *we* have them?') What do you predict the story is going to be about? Do you want to read on? Why?
- Recall/introduce a range of reading strategies and prompts appropriate to the group. What strategies can we use to help us read and understand an unfamiliar text?
- Share the lesson objective with the group. Ask the children, when reading, to record their predictions for the rest of the story and to say why.

INDEPENDENT READING

- Ask the children to read independently to page 21 ('You'd have thought they owned the river.').
- Prompt individual children to interact with the text. What did the elephants do when they were tired? What made Mango sometimes turn the right way up? Do you think the story is believable? Why? Why did the population of crocodiles increase?
- Review predictions. What do you think will happen next? Why?
- Ask the children to continue to read to page 24 ('And what she saw was Sneaker.').
- Prompt individual children to interact with the text. How did Mango get her own back on Sneaker? Mango, Wallow, Sneaker – why do you think the characters have these names?

RETURNING TO THE TEXT AND RESPONSE

- Support discussion. Clarify points raised and review reading strategies.
- Ask the children, in pairs, to summarise the story so far. Did anyone manage to jot down any questions to Mango and Rollo?
- Analyse the text. Divide a page in your reading journals. In pairs, skim read back through the text from page 19, ('For Mango and her cousin Rollo …') to page 21 ('… out of the river to rest on the bank.') and note down the advantages and disadvantages of living in the river for Mango. What evidence is there that Mango is content with her life in the river? What tells us that her life is going to change?
- Personal response. If you had to choose your favourite part of the story so far, which would you choose and why? Are you keen to read on? Explain your reasons.

FOLLOW-UP

- In preparation for Lesson 2, ask the children to continue reading to page 27 ('"Come on," she whispered …"Let's explore."') and jot down in their reading journals their predictions for the rest of the story and why.

Writing

- In reading journals, ask the children to invent short explanations stating why the following characters have their particular names: Mango, Gumbo, Rollo and Billow.
- Alternatively, sketch and label a scene from the story so far.

Speaking and listening

- 'You've probably wondered why leopards have spots.' In pairs, make up a story to explain this phenomenon, and present it to the rest of the group or the class. Use notes if required.

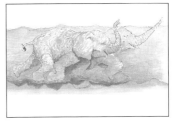

Synopsis:
Why do elephants have such long noses? Long ago, elephants lived underwater and used their trunks as breathing tubes. But, when the rivers dried up and the crocodiles multiplied to the extent that rivers were no longer big enough for elephants and crocodiles, the elephants had to move out.

The Underwater Elephants   Linda Newbery

Guided Reading   Lesson 2   Standard

Genre-specific text features:

animals are characterised; animals are standard characters in fables; theme of animal survival and freedom; main character is an animal.

Key teaching objectives:

Y5 T3 T2 To identify the point of view from which a story is told and how this affects the reader's response.

Y5 T3 T3 To change point of view, e.g. tell incident or describe a situation from the point of view of another character or perspective.

INTRODUCTION AND STRATEGY CHECK

- Recap Lesson 1 and clarify any points raised. Check that the children have read to page 29 ('"Come on," she whispered ... "Let's explore."'). What are your predictions for the rest of the story? Why?
- **Analyse the text. Refer back to page 27.** What does the author mean when she writes '... crocodiles log-jammed the river in both directions ... the river seemed to bristle with teeth.' Why do you think the river 'bristles' with teeth?
- **Discuss the role of the narrator.** What 'person' is used to tell the story? (third) Who is telling the story? (omniscient narrator) What evidence can you find to support your view?
- Share the lesson objective with the group. Ask the children, when reading, to think about the role of the narrator. Does the narrator 'side' with any of the characters? Is the reader provided with an 'objective' view of events? Is the reader provided with a 'subjective' view?

INDEPENDENT READING

- Ask the children to read independently to the end of the story.
- Prompt individual children to interact with the text. What do you think 'gallumph' means? What do you think 'lollopy' means? On page 33, the author writes 'A floating log twitched and showed its teeth.' What does she mean?

RETURNING TO THE TEXT AND RESPONSE

- Support discussion. Clarify points raised and review reading strategies.
- Review the role of the narrator and discuss narrative perspective. Ask the children to skim read back through the text and locate any examples that demonstrate from which perspective the story is told. Does the narrator 'side' with any of the characters? What evidence can you find to support your answer? (e.g. page 22, 'You'd have thought they owned the river.'; page 24, 'But it was no use trying to explain fairness to Sneaker.') What difference do you think it makes who tells a story? When is the reader more likely to get an 'objective' or truthful account of events? When is the reader more likely to get a 'subjective' or biased account of events?
- Choose two children, one to assume the role of Mango and one to assume the role of Sneaker. Hot seat the two characters and compare the two different perspectives on events.
- **Personal response.** A fable is supposed to explain why something is like it is. How well do you think this fable does that job? What would be the moral of this story?

FOLLOW-UP

Writing

- Ask the children to imagine they are wise old Mango with children and grandchildren of their own. Write the 'Chronicle of the Elephant Family' to be passed on for generations to come.
- Alternatively, retell the story from the point of view of Sneaker.

Speaking and listening

- Ask the children to imagine that Sneaker has been put on trial for crimes against elephants. Create a class courtroom. Choose one child to be the prosecution lawyer and one to be Sneaker's defence lawyer. Choose one child to be Mango and give evidence. The rest of the class act as the jury.

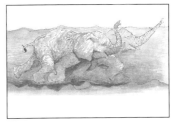

INTRODUCTION AND STRATEGY CHECK
- Recap Lesson 1 and clarify any points raised. Check that the children have read to page 27, ('"Come on," she whispered … "Let's explore."').
- Ask the children in pairs to summarise the story so far. What are your predictions for the rest of the story? Why?
- Discuss narrative perspective. Refer back to page 19 ('What stroke did they swim? Ellie-paddle!'). What do you notice about the text? What does this tell us about *who* is telling the story? (omniscient narrator) Why has the narrator chosen to comment at this point? What effect does this have on the reader? From whose perspective is the story told? Would the story read differently if it was told from another character's point of view? How?
- Share the lesson objective with the group. Ask the children, when reading, to think about how events would look if told from the point of view of Sneaker. Would the reader think differently about Sneaker?

INDEPENDENT READING
- Ask the children to read independently to page 32 ('The crocodile … would miss them.'). If they finish early, ask the children to write down five facts about Sneaker.
- Prompt individual children to interact with the text. How did Mango and Rollo keep cool? On page 29, the author writes 'His mud-grey sides were a shuddering mountain.' What do you think this means? On page 29, it says '… like dappled water'. What do you think this means?
- Read aloud the final paragraph of the story.

RETURNING TO THE TEXT AND RESPONSE
- Review the role of the narrator and discuss narrative perspective. What do you notice about the final paragraph? Why has the author chosen to comment at this point? In your view, is this technique effective? Why?
- Support discussion. Clarify points raised and review reading strategies.
- Discuss change in perspective. As a group, discuss how events might have looked if the story had been told by Sneaker. How would the reader have thought differently of Sneaker?
- Hot seat Sneaker. Ask the children to put questions to Sneaker. Respond in role.
- Personal response. Did you enjoy reading the story? Would you recommend it to anyone else? Why? Are you satisfied with the explanation given by the author as to why elephants have such long noses? What alternative explanation would you offer?

FOLLOW-UP
Writing
- Ask the children to imagine they are wise old Mango with children and grandchildren of their own. Write an account of elephant family history to be passed on for generations to come.
- Alternatively, in reading journals ask the children to invent short explanations stating why the following characters have their particular names: Sorrow, Sneaker and Wallow.

Speaking and listening
- Ask the children to imagine that Sneaker has been put on trial for crimes against elephants. Create a class courtroom. Choose one child to be the prosecution lawyer and one to be Sneaker's defence lawyer. Choose one child to be Mango and give evidence. The rest of the class act as the jury.

Synopsis:
Why do elephants have such long noses? Long ago, elephants lived underwater and used their trunks as breathing tubes. But, when the rivers dried up and the crocodiles multiplied to the extent that rivers were no longer big enough for elephants and crocodiles, the elephants had to move out.

TALK FOR WRITING/DRAMA

Communal voice

- In a group, ask the children to adopt the communal voice of Mango or Sneaker after the tail-biting incident, or of Billow, Mango's mother, at the end of the story. Each child, in turn, assumes the voice of the same character; the aim is to build up and develop an overall view of this character's opinions.

Debate

- The elephants were right to give up the river to the crocodiles. Who has the right to live in the river?

Quote unquote

- Locate and discuss examples from the text which demonstrate:
  - that Mango and Rollo enjoy playing in the river
  - that Mango is daring
  - that Sorrow likes to offer advice
  - that Sneaker is sneaky.

WRITING

- Imagine you are a naturalist who has been observing the behaviour of some underwater elephants. Write a field guide entry for 'Underwater Elephants In Focus' describing the behaviour of such elephants and how best to observe it. Use labelled diagrams to illustrate the guide.
- Using the introduction of the story as a model for writing, create a new fable. For example, 'You've probably wondered why cats always fall on their feet. Have they always done this? Don't they ever land on their backs?' Or, 'You've probably wondered why the sky is blue...'
- Transform one episode from the story into a cartoon strip. Use thought bubbles to indicate what the characters are thinking.
- Write a story illustrating the theme of survival.
- Imagine you are making 'The Underwater Elephants' into a film. Write notes on the opening sequence: directors' notes, music, images and voiceover. Include a storyboard to show how the action should develop.

Linda Newbery

About the Author

AUTHOR OF 'THE UNDERWATER ELEPHANTS' IN *THE ELEPHANT, THE HARE AND THE BLACK COBRA*

The idea behind the story of 'The Underwater Elephants' came from a recent theory that elephants once spent much of their time underwater, using their trunks as breathing tubes. This made me begin to think of a tale, rather like Rudyard Kipling's *Just So Stories*, which would explain this, and why elephants changed their ways to become land animals. I don't usually write stories about talking animals, but this was an exception, and one I really enjoyed writing about!

I enjoy writing for a range of ages. The writing process is much the same, and just as enjoyable, regardless of who the intended audience is. I have often found that one of the best things about writing for younger readers is that you don't have to stick to any one genre, but can write any kind of story you want to try. Most of my books are realistic novels about social issues, for older readers, but some of my most recent writing has led me into different areas.

I think that whatever you're writing, you have to really try and live in that story, live with those characters and see things through their eyes in order to make it work and make it real for the reader. I write stories by asking myself questions such as What if? Why? Who? I wonder whether…? I find that my stories come to me as I am trying to explain the answers to myself. This may take some time as the answers don't necessarily come at once. But the trick is to know which questions to ask, and to keep asking them until you get the answers you are happy with!

You can find a link to my website at www.storystreet.co.uk/streetwise/authors.

Awards
- *The Shell House* was shortlisted for the Guardian Children's Book Award 2003 and the Carnegie Medal 2003.

Other books by Linda Newbery you might also enjoy:
- *Blitz Boys, World War II Flashbacks*, A & C Black
- *Whistling Jack,* Harper Collins, Red Storybook
- *The Shell House,* David Fickling Books
- *The Damage Done,* Scholastic
- *No Way Back,* Orchard
- *Sisterland,* David Fickling Books

Brown Hare and the Fox   Martin Waddell

Guided Reading   Lesson 1   Standard

Genre-specific text features:

readers are encouraged to sympathise and be respectful towards the animals, theme of animal survival, freedom and the wild.

Key teaching objective:

Y5 T3 T8 To record predictions, questions, reflections while reading, e.g. through the use of a reading journal.

INTRODUCTION AND STRATEGY CHECK

- Ask the children to read to page 37 ('"I don't mind that …"… next morning.'). What can you tell about the story? Can anyone predict what might happen in the rest of the story?
- Refer to page 37 ('"You'd have to go out …," Grannie said.'). What does this sentence tell us about Brown Hare and how she lives and behaves? What does it tell us about how animals affect what humans do?
- Share the lesson objective with the group. Ask the children, when reading, to focus on Brown Hare and, in their reading journals, to jot down examples from the text which demonstrate the relationship between the animal and its environment. How does Brown Hare live? What is causing her to behave in the ways that she does? What effect do the animals have on what the humans do and feel?
- Recall/introduce a range of reading strategies and prompts appropriate to the group. What strategies can we use to help us read and understand an unfamiliar text?

INDEPENDENT READING

- Ask the children to read independently to page 41 ('"Is that it? … all she does?"').
- Prompt individual children to interact with the text. What is meant by 'plantation trees'? On page 41, the author writes that Brown Hare 'wizzled and twizzled'. What do you think he means?

RETURNING TO THE TEXT AND RESPONSE

- Support discussion. Clarify points raised and review reading strategies.
- Discuss the relationship between the animal and its environment. What examples did you find which highlight how Brown Hare lives and behaves? (e.g. page 38, '"The way a hare … belong to her."'; '"She eats the crop … old Brown Hare?"'; '"Keep very still … show herself."') Why do you think she behaves in these ways? Summarise by establishing that animals live in harmony with their environment. Why do you think Martin Waddell included details of Brown Hare's habitat and behaviour? (to create natural setting, to make story believable, realism) What effect does this have on the reader? (more inclined to believe it, better able to imagine it)
- Discuss the effect the animals have on human behaviour. What examples did you find which highlight how Brown Hare affects the family's behaviour? (e.g. page 37, '"If you want … have to get up!"'; page 39, '"Keep quiet, … Hare."') Summarise by establishing that humans have to modify their normal behaviour in order to observe animals.
- Discuss the setting for the story. Where do you think the story is set? (Ireland) How do you know? (Banagher Lake) Establish that the story contains examples of Irish English. Identify examples. ('Mammy', 'Granda', 'Hold your wheesht!') What effect does including these words have on the reader? (realism, creates atmosphere, contextualises story)

FOLLOW-UP

- In preparation for Lesson 2, ask the children to continue reading to the end of page 42 ('…as it slinked…gorse at the edge of the field.').

Writing

- Ask the children to imagine Granda is still alive. Describe what he was like and what he would do during a typical day. Use your knowledge of Grannie Brennan to support your interpretation.
- Alternatively, in reading journals, devise ten questions about the text. Swap questions with a partner and answer your partner's questions.

Speaking and listening

- In pairs, ask the children to improvise a telephone conversation between Nora and a school friend which took place just before Nora made the trip to Grannie Brennan's house.

Brown Hare and the Fox   Martin Waddell

Guided Reading Lesson 1 Access

INTRODUCTION AND STRATEGY CHECK

- Read aloud to page 36 ('*That* didn't please Donal.').
- Ask one child to summarise the story so far. What type of story do you think this is? Why? What have you learned about the main characters?
- Ask the children to read to the line '"I don't mind that one bit," Donal said … but he *did* mind, next morning.' on page 36. Can anyone predict what might happen in the rest of the story? Read out the earlier line '"You'd have to go out …," Grannie said.') What does this sentence tell us about Brown Hare and how she lives and behaves? Why does she behave in this way?
- Share the lesson objective with the group. Ask the children, when reading, to focus on Brown Hare and, in their reading journals, to jot down any words or phrases which show how she lives and behaves. How does Brown Hare live? What is causing her to behave in the ways that she does?
- Recall/introduce a range of reading strategies and prompts appropriate to the group. What strategies can we use to help us read and understand an unfamiliar text?

INDEPENDENT READING

- Read independently to page 41 ('"Is that it?" Donal whispered. "Is that all she does?"').
- Prompt individual children to interact with the text. On page 36, the author writes '… but he *did* mind, next morning.' Why do you think Donal did mind being in the fields at dawn? Why has the author used italics?

RETURNING TO THE TEXT AND RESPONSE

- Support discussion. Clarify points raised and review reading strategies.
- Discuss Brown Hare and her environment. What words or phrases did you find which show how Brown Hare lives and behaves? (e.g. pages 37–38, '"The way a hare … belong to her."'; page 38, '"She eats the crop … old Brown Hare?"'; page 38, '"Brown Hare has her young ones hidden …"') Why do you think she behaves in these ways? Summarise by establishing that animals live in harmony with their environment. Why do you think Martin Waddell included details of Brown Hare's habitat and behaviour? (to create natural setting, to make story believable)
- Discuss the setting for the story. Establish that the story is set in Ireland. Highlight that the story contains examples of Irish English. Identify examples ('Mammy', 'Granda', 'Hold your wheest!') Why has the author chosen to include these examples? (more realistic, creates atmosphere)
- Personal response. Ask the children to jot down in their reading journals their predictions for the rest of the story. What do you predict will happen in the rest of the story? What makes you think this? Are you keen to read on? Explain your reasons.

FOLLOW-UP

- In preparation for Lesson 2, ask the children to continue reading to page 42, ('At first she saw nothing at all … move.').

Writing

- Ask the children to imagine they are Jack Rooney. Create a diary entry recording the damage done to your crops by Brown Hare. Indicate your feelings about the matter.
- Alternatively, in reading journals, compose five questions about the text. Swap questions with a partner and answer your partner's questions.

Speaking and listening

- Ask the children to improvise a dialogue between Nora and her Mammy which took place just before Nora made the trip to Grannie Brennan's house. Include Nora's views on what she expects to do on her trip.

Synopsis:
Nora and her younger brother Donal go and stay with Grannie Brennan in her house by the lake. One morning, at dawn, they go out into the fields to try and see Brown Hare. A fox appears and chases Brown Hare. The children watch as Brown Hare evades the fox and prevents it from eating her young.

Brown Hare and the Fox   Martin Waddell

Guided Reading   Lesson 2   Standard

Genre-specific text features:

readers are encouraged to sympathise and be respectful towards the animals, theme of animal survival, freedom and the wild.

Key teaching objectives:

Y5 T3 T8 To record predictions, questions, reflections while reading, e.g. through the use of a reading journal.

INTRODUCTION AND STRATEGY CHECK

- Recap Lesson 1 and clarify any points raised. Check that the children have read to the end of page 42 ('… as it slinked … gorse at the edge of the field.').
- Ask the children to read to the line '"I'd better be … his chickens."' on page 43. What have we learned about how foxes and hares live? Read out the line '"Foxes eat any mortal thing they can lay hold of," Grannie said.' What does this sentence tell us about how foxes live? Establish that foxes are predators; their natural instinct is to hunt and kill for survival.
- Share the lesson objective with the group. Ask the children, when reading, to search for clues and jot down any words or phrases which indicate how foxes and hares survive. Use quotations and page references where appropriate. How do Brown Hare and Fox survive? What information can you find about their natural instincts?
- Recall/introduce a range of reading strategies and prompts appropriate to the group. What strategies can we use to help us read and understand an unfamiliar text?

INDEPENDENT READING

- Ask the children to read independently to the end of the story.
- Prompt individual children to interact with the text. What is 'gorse'? What evidence can you find which suggests that Donal has 'lost interest'?

RETURNING TO THE TEXT AND RESPONSE

- Support discussion. Clarify points raised and review reading strategies.
- Discuss the role of natural instinct and survival. What examples did you find of natural instinct in action? (e.g. maternal instinct of Brown Hare – page 46, '"She let him see her … then she led him away from where her young ones were hid."'; predatory instinct of Fox – page 44, '"He has her scent …"') What do these examples tell us about how animals behave? (e.g. survival, feeding, protection of young) The fox wants to kill Brown Hare. Does this make him an 'evil' fox?
- Analyse the text. Skim read the text from page 43 ('Nora had gone pale.') to page 47 ('There was no sign of Brown Hare.'). What devices does the author use to create excitement and suspense? For example:
  - low, whispering voices (page 43, '"Look …," Nora whispered.')
  - a real sense of a 'chase' (page 44, 'Brown Hare was off, and so was the fox.')
  - repetition; short sentences (pages 45–46, 'They ran … and they ran …')
  - italicised words for emphasis (pages 45–46, '*this way … this way … that.*')
  - short questions (page 46, '"Will he catch her?"'; '"Will he eat her?"')
  - ellipsis, dramatic pause (page 47, 'And …')
  - creation of atmosphere (page 47, 'The moon rose, … stirred …, moved …').

FOLLOW-UP
Writing

- Ask the children to imagine they write for a nature journal. Write an article for *Irish Wildlife Spotter*, describing what the opportunities are for observing wildlife on Jack Rooney's farm. Use timetables, sketches and plans to enhance the article.
- Alternatively, imagine you are five-year-old Donal. In reading journals, write a letter to Mammy explaining how things are going at the Lake and your experience of watching Brown Hare at dawn.

Speaking and listening

- A live wildlife documentary is being filmed at Rooney's farm. In groups, assume the roles of presenter, Grannie Brennan, Nora, Donal and other spectators. Improvise a commentary on the fox and hare chase and conduct interviews between the presenter and various spectators.

INTRODUCTION AND STRATEGY CHECK

- Recap Lesson 1 and clarify any points raised. Check that the children have read to page 42 ('At first she saw nothing at all ... move.').
- Ask one child to summarise the story so far. What are your predictions for the rest of the story?
- Read aloud to the line '"I'd better be ... his chickens."' on page 43. What have we learned about how foxes and hares live? **Read out the line '"Foxes eat anything they can lay hold of," Grannie said.'** What does this sentence tell us about how foxes live? Establish that foxes are predators; their natural instinct is to hunt and kill for survival.
- Share the lesson objective with the group. Ask the children, when reading, to jot down any words or phrases which indicate how Brown Hare and the fox survive. What information can you find about their natural instinct for survival?
- Recall/introduce a range of reading strategies and prompts appropriate to the group. What strategies can we use to help us read and understand an unfamiliar text?

INDEPENDENT READING

- Ask the children to read independently to page 47 ('And ...'). If they finish early, ask the children to jot down in their reading journals their predictions for the rest of the story.
- Prompt individual children to interact with the text. Why does Brown Hare sniff at the air? (page 43) Why doesn't Brown Hare run away when she can smell Fox? (page 44)
- Briefly discuss predictions for the rest of the story.
- Select one child to read to the end of the story.

RETURNING TO THE TEXT AND RESPONSE

- Support discussion. Clarify points raised and review reading strategies.
- Discuss the role of natural instinct and survival. What words or phrases did you find which illustrate a natural instinct for survival? (e.g. maternal instinct of Brown Hare – page 44, '"She'll lead him away from her babies."'; predatory instinct of the fox – page 44, '"He has her scent, ..."') The fox wants to kill Brown Hare. Does this make him an 'evil' fox?
- Analyse the text. Explain that the author uses a number of narrative techniques. For example:
  - Refer to page 45 ('They ran ... *this way ... that*.'). Why does the author write parts of the sentence on different lines? What effect does this create? Why does the author use italics?
  - Refer to pages 47–48 ('The moon rose ... soft lap of the water.'). How does this paragraph make you feel? Why? What words and phrases make you feel like this?
  - Ask the children to skim read the last few paragraphs. How do your feelings change throughout the course of the action? How does the author make you feel like this?

FOLLOW-UP

Writing

- Ask the children to imagine they are writing an entry for an encyclopaedia of animals. Write a short paragraph describing the behaviour and habitat of the fox and Brown Hare. Use labelled diagrams and illustrations to enhance your paragraph.
- Alternatively, imagine you are Nora. In reading journals write a letter to Mammy explaining how things are going at the lake and your exciting experience of watching Brown Hare at dawn.

Speaking and listening

- A live wildlife documentary is being filmed at Rooney's farm. In pairs, one to assume the role of presenter, the other the role of guest spectator. Conduct an interview live at Jack Rooney's farm.

Synopsis:
Nora and her younger brother Donal go and stay with Grannie Brennan in her house by the lake. One morning, at dawn, they go out into the fields to try and see Brown Hare. A fox appears and chases Brown Hare. The children watch as Brown Hare evades the fox and prevents it from eating her young.

TALK FOR WRITING/DRAMA

Thought tracking

- Freeze-frame key incidents of the story and use the technique of thought tracking to reveal the character's thoughts at various points in the drama.
  - What might the characters be thinking when waiting for Brown Hare to appear?
  - What might the characters be thinking as they anxiously watch the chase?
  - Imagine Jack Rooney awoke in time to see Brown Hare appear in his cow field. What might he think?
  - What might the characters think upon Brown Hare's escape?

Debate

- **The fox hunted Brown Hare.** Should humans be allowed to hunt foxes? What is the difference between foxes hunting hares and humans hunting foxes?

Fact or opinion?

- Ask the children to use evidence from the text to decide whether the following statements are fact or opinion:
  - Jack Rooney helps Grannie Brennan.
  - Grannie Brennan is very happy living by the lake.
  - Donal gets on well with his sister Nora.
  - The fox has been trying to kill Brown Hare since last spring.
  - Donal's level of interest in Brown Hare changes.
- Ask the children to refer to the text and create their own facts and opinions.

WRITING

- Retell the story so that the focus of Grannie Brennan, Nora and Donal is to observe the fox rather than Brown Hare. Comment on the fox's need to survive rather than Brown Hare's.
- Imagine you are Grannie Brennan. Write a dialogue between yourself and Jack Rooney to take place the following day.
- Write and present a story about animals involving a chase of some kind.
- Imagine you are making a wildlife programme. Describe how you would present the behaviour of the hare and the fox.
- Summarise the story in no more than fifty words.

About the Author

AUTHOR OF 'BROWN HARE AND THE FOX' IN *THE ELEPHANT, THE HARE AND THE BLACK COBRA*

One cold morning in Clare I woke very early, and walked alone by the side of a lake. Why? I was on holiday there with my children, and that morning I just felt like being out on my own, that's why. The last thing I was expecting was that I'd find a story ... but I did.

Something moved in a field by the lake, then was still, seemed to quiver, then moved again quickly and was gone ... *hoppity-hoppity-hop* into the long grass. I stood very still, and watched. It reappeared, further up the field. Quiver ... *hoppity-hoppity-hop, this way and this way and this way and that* ... gone again, disappearing into the rocks and furze.

I'd just met Brown Hare, and I knew she was a *story* but I didn't know what sort of story. The words 'hoppity' and 'this way and that' were there from the beginning, tangled with the image, the remoteness, the dark green of the field and the bright light of dawn on the lake.

Sometimes people think writers are lazy, all that standing about in fields, doing nothing. But the *nothing* can quickly become *something* and churn about in the head, till the day comes when it wants to be written. It was years later that this one resurfaced. *Hoppity-hoppity-hop* and my writing mind was back in Clare, by the lake ... though in real life I was at my desk, in the stone barn by the sea, where I write my stories.

I started with the hare, and the cold morning in Clare ... that *ryhmes* ... and I thought of the beauty of the setting, with the lake flashing in the cold sunlight and ... and ... what then?

That's the trouble with being a writer. The words can be interesting, sometimes beautiful, but something has to *happen* to make it a story. There have to be characters in it ... someone to see Brown Hare, and think 'hoppity-hoppity-hoppity-hop'. Go with just the words, and you have a short descriptive poem that catches a beautiful moment. Stories need more than that. They need people, conflict, action, drama.

Off goes my mind *this way and this way and this way and that ....*

Hoppity-hoppity-hoppity-hop, that's how this story was written.

Awards
- *Can't You Sleep Little Bear?* won the Smarties Prize in 1988 and the Kate Greenaway Award in 1988.
- *Starry Night* was shortlisted for the Guardian Young Fiction Award.
- *Frankie's Story* was shortlisted for the Carnegie Award.

Other books by Martin Waddell you might also enjoy:
- *The Life and Loves of Zoe T Curly,* Walker Books
- *The Kidnapping of Susie Q,* Walker Books
- *Shooting Star,* Walker Books
- *The Orchard Book of Ghostly Stories,* Orchard
- *The Dump Gang,* Walker Books
- *Fred the Angel,* Walker Books

Martin Waddell also writes for the *Genre Range* strand of *Literacy Land* and the *Longman Book Project*.

Compare, Contrast and Connect

STYLES AND TECHNIQUES

Setting

- The settings in the three animal short stories contrast with one another. Compare and contrast two of the settings: for example, 'Rikki-Tikki-Tavi' and 'Brown Hare and the Fox'; the Indian jungle and a mountainside in Ireland.

Writing

- Ask the children to compare the two settings. Draw up a comparison grid using quotations from the texts and explain inferences made. How do the settings differ?

Author's choices

- Consider the options a writer is faced with when writing an animal story. For example:
  - Should the animals speak? Should they narrate the story? Should they speak to humans or just to other animals?
  - Should the animals behave like animals? Should they be anthropomorphic?
  - Should the animals be understood by humans or just by other animals?
  - Should humans play a role in the story? Should they speak or only observe?
- Review all three short stories and ask the children to jot down the techniques each writer has chosen. Why do you think the writers have made these choices?

Writing

- Ask the children to write an animal story using one or more of the techniques used in these stories. Why did you make these choices? Are you satisfied with the outcome?

THEMES

Nature

- Nature is a theme that runs throughout all three short stories.
- Discuss the subject of habitat. Compare and contrast the natural causes which force Rikki-tikki, Mango and Brown Hare to leave their homes. Why do you think the writers might have included these events?
- Compare and contrast the ways in which Rikki-tikki, Mango and Brown Hare fight for survival. Who saves himself? Who saves others?
- Contrast how Mango and Rikki-tikki must adapt to their new surroundings.
- Discuss who the 'predators' are in these stories. Who is the 'prey'? Explain the reasons for your judgements.

Rescue

- Analyse the theme of rescue in all three stories. Think about: Who? What? Why? When? How? In what ways do the rescues differ?
  - Debate. Nag and the fox – villains or victims? Rikki-tikki and Mango – heroes?

Compare, Contrast and Connect

Respect and affection
- Explore the theme of respect and affection in all three of the stories. Consider: respect for animals by animals; for animals by humans; for humans by animals and for humans by humans.
  - **Compare how Rikki-tikki and Mango show respect to other animals. Contrast with how Nag and Sneaker show respect to other animals.** Are Nag and Sneaker responsible for their actions?
  - **Compare and contrast how Teddy and his family and Donal, Nora and Grannie Brennan show affection for Rikki-tikki and the Brown Hare.** In what ways do they display affection?
  - **Compare how humans treat other humans.** How do Teddy's family regard each other? Compare with how Donal's family regard each other.
  - **Compare Teddy's mother and Nora.** In what ways are these characters similar? How do they regard the animals? Why?

CHARACTERS
- On a scale of 1–5, ask the children to rank the major animal characters against set criteria, using the texts to justify their choice: for example, weak, strong, kind, cruel and adventurous.
- Ask the children to discuss the following questions with reference to the texts:
  - Which characters are similar? In what ways?
  - Who is the strongest character? Why?
  - Which characters would get on well? Why?
  - Which character would you trust? Why?
  - Whom do you empathise with?
  - Whom do you admire the most? Why?
  - Which character would you own as a pet? Why?
  - Which character is the cleverest? Why?
  - Who are the heroes? Who are the victims?

CLASSIC VERSUS CONTEMPORARY
- Ask the children to investigate the differences in language between 'Rikki-Tikki-Tavi' and another text. Look at the different registers, or levels of formality, in the narration.
  - Which story is more formal?
  - If written today, would 'Rikki-Tikki-Tavi' read differently?
  - How does the formality of the language affect the reader? Does it make a difference when reading to yourself or listening to the story being read?

Writing
- Ask the children to find and list examples of language use, both at sentence and word level, which affect the stories' register: for example, the use of contracted forms, e.g. 'weren't', 'can't' or 'don't', or of specific vocabulary.

PERSONAL RESPONSE
- Organise the class into groups and allocate one of the short stories to each group. Write a composite review representing the views of the group. Nominate an 'envoy' to share the response with another group.

Independent / Whole Class Reading

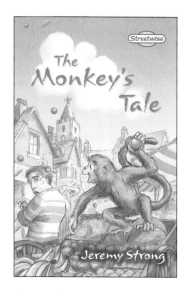

Synopsis:

Ziggy the monkey escapes from the pet shop, causing chaos. He finds his way to the woods at the edge of town, and lives off the apples in a nearby orchard. The owner of the orchard doesn't see Ziggy, but two children do – Jess and Daniel. They can't catch him, though. As the weather changes and the nights draw in, life in the woods starts to get more difficult for Ziggy – until he is saved by Jess and Daniel.

TWENTY QUESTIONS

Chapter 1	From what we learn in this chapter, what can we say about the character of Ziggy? How would you describe his appearance and personality?
Chapter 1	Why do you think Ziggy wanted to escape from Mr Luke's shop?
Chapter 1	Imagine you are the old lady with the poodle. What would be your view of events?
Chapter 2	What does the title of the second chapter mean? Why has the author used this title?
Chapter 2	When you were reading this chapter, did you hope that Ziggy would get away from Mr Luke? Why?
Chapter 3	After trying so hard to escape, why does Ziggy think about his cage again at the beginning of the third chapter?
Chapter 3	Describe Ziggy's emotions during his first few days living in the wood. How do they compare with his feelings in the pet shop? How have they changed? Where do you think he would prefer to live?
Chapter 3	What problems will Ziggy face when winter comes?
Chapter 4	Describe the characters of Daniel and Jess. What roles do you think they will play in the rest of the story?
Chapter 4	Why does the children's mother not believe their story about the monkey?
Chapter 4	Review the problems that Ziggy faces in this chapter. Describe how his feelings change towards living in the wood. Where would he prefer to live now – the wood or the pet shop?
Chapter 5	Why does Ziggy think that he will find nuts in the ground? Why doesn't he find any?
Chapter 5	What do you think would have happened to Ziggy if he hadn't found the bread on the bird table? What else could he have found to eat?
Chapter 6	Why do Daniel, Jess and their mother want to catch Ziggy?
Chapter 6	Why is it that the traps that Daniel and his father set for Ziggy do not work?
Chapter 7	Look to see how Ziggy's eyes are described in this chapter. How does this compare with how they were earlier in the story? Why have they changed?
Chapter 7	Why doesn't Ziggy try to escape from Jess?
Chapter 8	How do you think Ziggy feels about living in the house? Do you think he prefers it to living in the wood? Why? Do you think he will feel the same way when summer returns?
Chapter 8	Imagine how Jess and Daniel feel about Ziggy living in their home. How does this compare with how their Mum and Dad feel about it? Why?
Overview	What devices does the author use to show the differing relationships between Ziggy and the human characters in the story?

TALK FOR WRITING/DRAMA

If using the text with a group or as a class novel

- **Hot seating.** Hot seat one or more of the characters at various points in the novel. For example, hot seat Daniel when he first tries, unsuccessfully, to catch Ziggy, or Mr Luke immediately after Ziggy's escape.
- **Oral storytelling.** Retell the story around the group or the class, taking it in turns to add two sentences.
- **Debate.** Should animals be caged and kept in zoos?
- **Hypothetical happenings.** Discuss 'What ifs':
  - What if Ziggy hadn't escaped?
  - What if Daniel had succeeded in catching Ziggy?
  - What if the apple farmer had realised why his apples were disappearing?
  - What if Daniel and Jess's parents didn't want to keep Ziggy?
  - What if…? (Create your own examples.)

RESPONSE TO THE TEXT

As ongoing work in reading journals

- Illustrate one of the scenes described in Chapter 1. Use evidence from the text to support your interpretation.
- Rewrite Chapter 4 from the point of view of Daniel or Jess.
- Write a headline and the opening paragraph of a front page newspaper story about the monkey escaping from the pet shop.
- Create a comic strip of the main events in the story.
- Imagine you are Daniel or Jess. Write a letter to Mr Luke thanking him for allowing you to keep Ziggy and telling him about some of the monkey's recent adventures.
- Write another adventure for Ziggy the monkey in the style of Jeremy Strong. In what other ways does Ziggy's sense of mischief return?

Synopsis:

When Chrissie argues with her father about her exams, she gets so angry that she leaves home. Sheeka, her dog, goes with her. For a while, Chrissie and Sheeka are happy living a travelling life together, until fate conspires to separate them. Meanwhile, Chrissie's younger sister Polly travels to Italy with her stepmother Emilia, to visit Nona, Emilia's mother. On a visit to Assisi to ask for the help of St Francis in finding Sheeka, they are almost killed in an earthquake. In the end, everyone is reunited.

TWENTY QUESTIONS

Chapter 1	From whose point of view is the first part of this chapter written? How would you describe the emotions that this character is feeling?
Chapter 1	From whose point of view is the second part of this chapter written? What emotions is this character feeling? How do they differ from those of the first character? Why?
Chapter 1	What do we learn about the character of Dad in this chapter? What role do you think he will play in the rest of the novel?
Chapter 1	What do we learn about the character of Chrissie in this chapter? How does it differ, depending on whose point of view we are hearing?
Chapter 2	Why do you think Chrissie doesn't want to go to university?
Chapter 2	Look at the way Dog-Dog speaks to Sheeka in this chapter. How does his way of speaking differ from hers? What can we infer about him from this? What else can we say about his character?
Chapter 2	Imagine you are Chrissie. What are your feelings towards Dad at this point? Towards Polly? Towards Sheeka?
Chapter 3	In the early part of this chapter, we hear how Sheeka 'pleads with her eyes' to Chrissie. What do you think this means? How does Sheeka look when she is doing this? How does Chrissie react? Why?
Chapter 3	If Sheeka were a person, what sort of person would she be? What would she look like? How would she act? Would you describe Sheeka's actions in this chapter as 'out of character'? Why?
Chapter 3	What do we learn about the character of Pamela Norris in this chapter? What role do you think she will play in the rest of the novel?
Chapter 4	In this chapter, we hear how Polly and Emilia blame themselves for Chrissie having run away. Do you think they are right to do this? Why? If not, who is to blame? Why?
Chapter 4	What does Pamela infer about Sheeka in this chapter? Why? Is she right?
Chapter 4	Do you think Pamela would normally talk to travellers with dogs? Why?
Chapter 5	What do we learn about the character of Nona in this chapter? What role do you think she will play in the rest of the novel?
Chapter 5	Do you think Nona really believes in miracles? Does Polly?
Chapter 5	Why does Polly think the young man on the scooter is 'rather wonderful'?
Chapter 6	What makes Sheeka feel terrible when she wakes up at the start of this chapter?
Chapter 7	Do you think Sheeka knows that Chrissie is in the other car? How can she know this? If she doesn't know, why does she act in the way she does?
Chapter 7	Compare the characters of Chrissie and Pamela. Does it surprise you that they become 'firm friends'? Why?
Chapter 7	Describe the relationship between Chrissie and her dad at the end of the novel. How has it changed? What has made it change?
Overview	How does the author encourage us to see events from different perspectives? Is she successful in doing this?

Novel Ideas

TALK FOR WRITING/DRAMA

If using the text with a group or as a class novel

- **Freeze-frame.** Retell through drama one or more chapters of the story. Perform for an audience and freeze-frame key incidents, for example, when Sheeka runs away or when the earthquake happens. Record the still images on digital camera and capture onto presentation software such as PowerPoint to create an electronic storyboard. Use as a tool for organising writing.
- **Improvisation.** Improvise a discussion between Sheeka's dog friends about possible reasons for her disappearance.
- **Debate.** Was it right for Chrissie to miss taking her A levels?
- **Hypothetical happenings.** Discuss 'What ifs':
  - What if Pamela Norris hadn't found Sheeka?
  - What if Polly had been killed in the earthquake?
  - What if Sheeka had run away from Pamela?
  - What if Dave hadn't dropped his wallet in the petrol station?
  - What if…? (Create your own examples.)

RESPONSE TO THE TEXT

As ongoing work in reading journals

- Using evidence from Chapter 1, sketch and label Chrissie on the night she ran away.
- Imagine a correspondence between Chrissie and Polly after Chrissie has run away. Write a series of letters between the two characters.
- Using evidence from the text, design a 'Missing' poster for Chrissie.
- Imagine you are Chrissie's dad. Write diary entries covering key events in the story.
- Create titles for the seven chapters.
- How was the conflict resolved? Write an additional chapter for the story.

Independent / Whole Class Reading

Synopsis:

Ant, an English schoolboy, travels to Brazil to visit a farm belonging to his stepfather. He befriends a local boy, Pedrinho, and together they pay a visit to Pedrinho's 'friends' the alligators. The alligators are in danger from poachers, and it seems that Alberto, the farm manager, might be involved in the poaching in some way. However, Alberto, Ant and Pedrinho end up saving the alligators from poachers.

TWENTY QUESTIONS

Chapter 1	What do we learn in this chapter about the relationship between Ant and Luis? How do they act towards each other? Why do they do this? What do they really think of each other?
Chapter 2	What do we learn in the first two chapters about Alberto? What do we know to be true about him? What do we think might be true about him? Why?
Chapter 4	How would you describe the relationship between Ant and his mother? What is her attitude towards him? Why do you think this is?
Chapters 4 and 5	Imagine you are Ant. What are your first impressions of Pedrinho? Do these change after your initial meeting with him? Why?
Chapter 5	Who do you think Pedrinho means by his 'friends'?
Chapters 6, 7 & 8	Compare and contrast the attitudes of Ant and Pedrinho towards the Brazilian wildlife. Why are they so different? What do you think Pedrinho would think of English wildlife?
Chapter 9	When reading this chapter, what do you think has happened to Amarela the alligator? Why is she not with the other two alligators?
Chapter 10	Has your opinion of Alberto changed by this point in the story? Why? Has your view of the role he will play in the rest of the story changed?
Chapter 11	At first, Luis seems reluctant to believe Ant's story about goings-on in the barn. Why do you think this is?
Chapter 12	What is our view of Alberto by the end of this chapter? Why? Has your view of the role he will play in the rest of the story changed? If so, how?
Chapter 13	How has Ant's attitude to the Brazilian environment and wildlife changed since he first arrived in the Pantanal? Why?
Chapter 14	Why do you think Pedrinho believes Amarela is dead? Do you believe she is dead at this point? Why?
Chapter 15	How would you describe the relationship between Pedrinho and Amarela? Do you think it would be possible in real life for a boy to befriend an alligator?
Chapter 16	What are your first impressions of the two policemen? What do you think their role will be in the rest of the story? Why?
Chapter 17	What is the weather like during this chapter? How does this contribute to the atmosphere?
Chapter 18	Imagine you are Ant's mother. What are your thoughts and feelings as your son runs off with Pedrinho?
Chapter 19	Compare and contrast the characters of Batista and Oliveira. How are they similar? How do they differ?
Chapter 20	Describe how Pedrinho might feel when he realises the hideout has not been a secret from Alberto.
Chapter 21	Compare the gifts that Ant and Pedrinho give to each other. In your view, which is the better gift? Which will be most treasured? Why?
Overview	Who, in your view, is the hero of this story? Why?

Novel Ideas

TALK FOR WRITING/DRAMA

If using the text with a group or as a class novel

- **Decision alley/thought tunnel.** At various points in the story, Ant must make decisions. For example, should he cross the river with Pedrinho? Should he believe that Alberto is a poacher? **Select a child to take on the role of Ant. Ask the children to form two lines opposite each other to create the 'alley' or 'tunnel'.** As Ant walks through the tunnel, take it in turns to offer advice on the course of action he should take. **Alternatively, after Ant's first trip to the alligator swamp with Pedrinho, make the two lines represent the two sides of his conscience.** Each side of the alley states what Ant is thinking.
- **Role on the wall.** Sketch one of the characters from the story and surround with information about that character. For example, sketch Luis and surround him with facts derived from the text. **If dramatising the story, additional facts and information can be added during the drama, including the children's and other characters' opinions of Luis.**
- **Debate.** Pedrinho's life in Brazil is better than Ant's life in England.
- **Hypothetical happenings.** Discuss 'What ifs':
  - What if Alberto had been guilty?
  - What if the policemen had caught Ant and Pedrinho?
  - What if Amarela had knocked out Pedrinho with her tail?
  - What if Pedrinho had gone back to Britain with Luis and Ant?
  - What if…? (Create your own examples.)

RESPONSE TO THE TEXT

As ongoing work in reading journals

- Using evidence from Chapters 1 and 2, sketch and label Alberto.
- Using evidence from the text, compare the lives of Ant and Pedrinho. How are they different?
- Make notes on the character of Ant. How does his character change over the course of his stay?
- Retell Chapter 7 from the point of view of Pedrinho.
- Imagine you are Ant. Write a letter to a friend describing your stay in Brazil.
- Imagine you are Luis. Transcribe the two-way radio conversation between you and your cousin, the Chief Inspector in the state capital.

TEXT FEATURES

In discussing animal stories, some of the following textual features could be noted:

- Located in all animal, or human and animal world.
- Animals are characterised – as animals or anthropomorphic (animals taking on human characteristics).
- Communication might involve spoken language: animals understood by humans, by other animals, or both.
- Point of view can be animal or human.
- Often feature environmental, ecological or moral issues: protection of habitat, cruelty, experimentation, the call of the wild, the hunter and the hunted.
- The bond between humans and animals is often central to the story.
- Sometimes centre on working animals: sheepdogs, guide dogs, seaside donkeys.
- Often explore the relationship between humans and pets.
- Imagery often concerns wildness, freedom, domesticity.
- Plot often involves humans 'saved' by, or brought up by, animals.

EXPLORATION OF THE GENRE

Key questions

- Can an animal story also belong to another genre, e.g. animal ghost stories?
- Can an animal story deal with any issue or just animal issues?
- Is an animal story sometimes more a story about humans?
- How can animal stories be used to convey social or environmental issues?
- Can animal stories appeal to boys and girls equally?
- Can a story be called an animal story if its central character is not an animal?
- Do animal stories have to assume that animals have human language?
- What generalisations can you make about animal stories?

Possible activities

- Explore other animal texts, e.g. cartoons, reference books, websites, CD-ROMs.
- Research issues surrounding animals. Choose one issue and make a cartoon strip to tell others about the issue.
- Discuss the valuable contributions animals can make to individuals and groups. Devise a story to show this contribution to others.
- Make observations of animals you know, for example, pets, pets of friends or neighbours and wild animals in your garden. Write notes about the animal, then share notes with a partner and write a story featuring both animals.
- Create a fact file about an animal to put into a story. Include details such as its favourite food, its habitat and how anthropomorphically it will be presented.
- Talk about which animal characters you remember from stories when you were younger. Discuss how animals were presented in those stories.
- Make a list of any other animal stories you have read with recommendations about who might enjoy them and why.

WIDER READING

- **Animal Ark/Dolphin Diaries,** Lucy Daniels
  Hodder Children's Books
  An ever-growing series of stories featuring animals and the bond they forge with humans.

- **Love that Dog,** Sharon Creech
  Longman; ISBN: 0582796636
  Jack doesn't write poems _ 'Can't do it. Brain's empty.' But Miss Stretchberry persuades
  him to write one, then another and another. And soon Jack comes to understand poetry, to
  love it and to use it to express something that he hasn't been able to talk about – the death
  of his dog.

- **The Last Wolf,** Michael Morpurgo
  Corgi Children's; ISBN: 0440865077
  As he convalesces from a bout of pneumonia, Michael McLeod learns to use a computer and
  uses it to research his family tree. From a distant cousin, he receives the story of an ancestor,
  Robbie McLeod. An orphan, Robbie is caught up in the Jacobite Rebellion and survives the
  battle of Culloden. However, he is a fugitive from the English army and must live wild in the
  Highlands. There he meets a wolf cub, itself an orphan, and son of what was supposedly the
  last wolf in Scotland. Robbie and the wolf manage to journey to America where each makes
  a new life for himself.

- **The Sheep-Pig,** Dick King-Smith
  Puffin Modern Classics; ISBN: 0141302801
  When Farmer Hogget wins a piglet in a guess-the-weight competition, he plans to turn it
  into bacon and ham. However, Fly the collie takes the pig under her wing, learns that his
  name is Babe, and teaches him the way of the sheepdog. Babe lacks the speed of a dog, but
  makes up for it with a revolutionary new technique – being polite to the sheep. This helps
  him to win the Grand Challenge Sheep Dog Trials.

- **Watership Down,** Richard Adams
  Puffin Books; ISBN: 0140306013
  Fiver the rabbit foresees the destruction of his warren. He and his brother Hazel persuade a
  group of friends to leave in search of a new home. They journey across country, surviving a
  variety of both natural and man-made perils, and find a seemingly ideal hilltop home.
  However, the group are all males. In order for their new warren to survive, they have to help
  some females to escape from Efrafa, a neighbouring warren run along military lines.

- **The Wind in the Willows,** Kenneth Grahame
  Penguin Popular Classics; ISBN: 0140621229
  One spring morning, Mole goes for a walk and meets up with Rat. Together, they go for a
  boat trip and a picnic and a friendship is forged. They meet up with Mr Toad, the lovable
  rogue, who owns Toad Hall. Toad has a weakness for fast cars which gets him into trouble
  and even lands him in prison. While he's away, Toad Hall is seized by the Stoats and Weasels
  and, together with his friends Mole, Rat and Badger, Toad must hatch a plan to get it back.

AUTHOR OF *OLGA'S OGGIES*

If you want to be a good writer you have to be a reader first.

Reading is one of my favourite things. I love reading history and crime fiction best.

I have always made up stories in my head, and for many years, that is where they stayed – running inside my head like my own technicolour films! So, if you get in trouble for daydreaming when really you are just imagining the stories in your head coming to life, perhaps you're destined to become a famous author!

If you can't think of anything to write about when you have to write stories, a good tip is to ask yourself 'What if I took an ordinary situation and added a bit of magic?'

I live in Plymouth and when I wrote *Olga's Oggies,* I set the story in the primary school that my children attended – with a different name, of course. I visit a lot of local schools and children always love to hear stories about places they recognise, which is why I often set my books in Plymouth.

When I wrote *Olga's Oggies*, I asked myself, 'What if a school child could magically make time stand still? What would she do?' Most of my life I have worked with children and so I combined elements of different characters together to get the character of Olga. Olga has actually had a lot more adventures with her magic oggies, where she did much naughtier things, but I'll leave those up to the reader to imagine!

If you enjoyed reading *Olga's Oggies*, why not try *I Have a Plan*, which is another adventure story, or *Skulduggery*, which is a detective story where the boy hero solves the crime.

Other books by Anne Adeney you might also enjoy:

* *Skulduggery,* Orion
* *Una's Spelling Test,* Oxford University Press
* *Grizzlegrump's Revenge*, Oxford University Press
* *First Leaf Festival*, Oxford University Press
* *Boring Old Bed*, Reed
* *I Have a Plan*, Chivers
* *True Adventures*, Scripture Union

AUTHOR OF 'RICKY'S WHEELS' IN *RICKY, KARIM AND SPIT NOLAN* AND *STRANDED!*

I really enjoyed writing my *Streetwise* stories because it involved a perfect mix of interesting research, happy memories and making things up.

I used the Internet to research my story, 'Ricky's Wheels'. I found a writer called Gary Karp, who has been in a wheelchair since his teens. I read his book, *Life on Wheels* and emailed him with questions I still had about what Ricky would be able to do and how he would do it.
In my original idea, Sam was going to push Ricky up the hills and jump on the back of his wheelchair as they were both coming down. However, Gary told me that that wouldn't work because the wheelchair would overbalance, and anyway Ricky would be perfectly capable of wheeling uphill on his own. When I had finished the story, Gary read it for me to make sure it was believable.

The idea for *Stranded!* came from my own childhood, when my family had a caravan on Hayling Island very close to a muddy creek. One time, my sister and our cousin tried to cross the creek, but the mud in the middle was much deeper than they had expected. Then we noticed the tide was coming in … It was absolutely terrifying!

I haven't been back to Hayling Island since I was eight, so I decided to set the story on the Norfolk coast, which I've visited more recently. I read about salt marshes on the Internet to refresh my memories before I started writing.

I love reading and writing. I don't enjoy writing or reading long passages of description because I'm quite an impatient person. I'm also rather reckless, so I tend to jump in with both feet – and then panic! I guess that's why my characters often have to find ways of overcoming fear and solving problems.

If you have enjoyed reading 'Ricky's Wheels' and *Stranded!* you might also like *Pedal Power: Land's End to John o' Groats* as it has lots of geography in a short diary format, which could give you some ideas for settings when you are writing stories of your own.

Awards
- *Pedal Power: Lands End to John o'Groats* was selected for the Child Education and Junior Education 'Best Books in 2002' supplement.

Other books by Jenny Alexander you might also enjoy:
- *Haunting for Beginners,* Puffin
- *The Good Ghost Guide, Pelican Hilo,* Longman
- *Pedal Power: Land's End to John o'Groats, Info Trail*, Longman
- *Bullies, Bigmouths and So-Called Friends,* Hodder

Jenny Alexander also writes for the *Story Street, Genre Range* and *Info Trail* strands of *Literacy Land* and *Pelican Hilos*.

About the Author

AUTHOR OF 'KISSY, KISSY' IN *BURGLARS, DUCKS AND KISSING FROGS* AND *BUTCH THE CAT-DOG*

I've always loved writing. When I was about 10, Mr Padgett, the Headmaster of my primary school, read out one of my ghost stories to the class. When he finished, he said, "Well, I don't know about anyone else, but it certainly scared me!" and I thought, "Yes! That's what I want to do for the rest of my life – tell stories!" Now, years later, and with more than 60 published books to my name, I'm still doing it.

I had terrific fun writing my two humorous *Streetwise* stories. 'Kissy, Kissy' was inspired by the traditional tale of 'The Frog Prince', but I gave the story a twist and added a new character – Grandma Glugga, who rules the Palace Pond and says ludicrous things like "Ponk me for a slug-sniggler!" (No, I don't know what she means, either!)

As for *Butch the Cat-Dog*... I absolutely love cats, and include them in a lot of my stories, so the chance to write a whole book about one was irresistible. I'm thankful to say that, except for his ginger colour, Tigger/Butch isn't based on any of my own cats! But I had a lot of catty help with the noises he makes!

If you've enjoyed my *Streetwise* tales, then you might also want to read *Sea Horses*, which is set on the Cornish coast, where I live, and tells the story of a broken statue, an ancient curse, and a strange white pony.

You can find a link to my website at www.storystreet.co.uk/streetwise/authors. You can get the news of my latest projects, and read "taster" chapters from my books.

Awards
* *Short and Scary!* is in the Red House Awards Top 100 for 2003.
* *Demon Crossing* was runner up in both the Angus Council Children's Book Awards 2002 and the Askews Torchlight Award 2002.

Other books by Louise Cooper you might also enjoy:
* *Sea Horses 1,* Puffin – (3 more to follow)
* *Short and Scary!,* Oxford University Press
* *Demon Crossing,* Hodder Children's
* *Hunter's Moon,* Hodder Children's
* *The Daughter of Storms trilogy,* Hodder Children's:
    * *1 - Daughter of Storms*
    * *2 - The Dark Caller*
    * *3 - Keepers of Light*
* *The Mirror, Mirror series,* Hodder Children's:
    * *1 – Breaking Through*
    * *2 – Running Free*
    * *3 – Testing Limits*

About the Author

AUTHOR OF *THE SECRET OF MONKS ISLAND*

My approach to writing is to think of a place or a person to help spark off an idea. Sometimes the plot comes from the characters themselves as I develop them. I try to make the characters come to life because I feel if the reader can't 'see' the characters, then the story will be a flop.

As I am writing the plot, I try to make the main character change for the better in some way, or grow during the story. At the beginning of *The Secret of Monks Island*, Sam is tired of her elder sister always stealing the limelight, but by the end of the story, Sam is the heroine as she proves how brave and resourceful she can be.

When I am writing I often choose a place or a setting I know well. However the setting for the story *The Secret of Monks Island* is in the North-East of England and I must confess, I have never been there, so this meant doing some historical research. I have local friends who know the area well and they helped me by providing maps and photographs to help get me started. I also went to my local library to read about the history of the area and about the Viking and Anglo-Saxon influences, and luckily for me, one of my local friends is a retired schoolteacher who knows quite a lot about the Vikings and Anglo-Saxons.

The spotted dog in the story is based on a dalmatian I know and my own springer spaniel, who loves swimming and who I can well imagine digging up hidden treasures!

If you have enjoyed reading *The Secret of Monks Island*, you might also like *River of Secrets* which is a mystery about a girl who discovers some dangerous secrets.

Awards
* *Revenge of the Wildcat* was a runner up in a competition for BBC Scotland and Kelpie Books and was also serialised on the radio.

Other books by Griselda Gifford you might also enjoy:
* *Revenge of the Wildcat*, Canongate
* *The Skeleton Upstairs*, Oxford University Press
* *Trapped!*, Macmillan Education
* *Ben's Expedition*, Bodely Head
* *River of Secrets*, Andersen Press
* *Second Sight*, Andersen Press

AUTHOR OF 'BURGLARS' IN *BURGLARS, DUCKS AND KISSING FROGS*

Norman Hunter wrote the first Professor Branestawm stories for BBC radio. They were broadcast in the early 1930s. The first Professor Branestawm book, *The Incredible Adventures of Professor Branestawm*, was published in 1933. The story 'Burglars' comes from that book.

Norman Hunter was born in 1899 in London. He didn't enjoy school and when the First World War broke out in 1914 he volunteered to join the army. After the war he had three jobs: he learned to type and worked in advertising, he was a magician in the theatre, and he became a successful writer. He worked in South Africa for 20 years, then retired to live in London. He died in 1995.

This is how Norman Hunter described his life:

> I was born in London, 1899, a few years after the other Normans got there. After escaping from school I had a course in all-in wrestling with typewriters and eventually inserted my self into the advertising profession. I used to write advertisements of such allure that people bought vast quantities of the most unlikely things before they could stop themselves. I am also a conjuror, and managed to let off two hundred performances at Maskelyne and Devant's Theatre of Magic before the Nazis bombed my venue. By then I was in Bournemouth, but came back to London in time to be chased out again by flying bombs and finished the war living on a motor yacht on the Thames.

There are 16 books about Professor Branestawm, but some of them are out of print. The professor is an absent-minded inventor who wears five pairs of glasses at once (one pair to look for the others when he loses them!) His inventions include a paint-on carpet and machines for making pancakes, stroking cats and finding lost property. He is looked after by Mrs Flittersnoop, his sensible cook and housekeeper. His best friend is Colonel Dedshott of the Catapault Cavaliers, "a very brave gentleman who never missed a train, an enemy or an opportunity to get into trouble".

Norman Hunter's writing shows how he loved to play with words. In the book *Professor Branestawm's Dictionary*, the Professor invents his own definitions (for example, 'abominable – a piece of explosive swallowed by a male cow').

Other books by Norman Hunter you might also enjoy:
- *The Incredible Adventures of Professor Branestawm,* Puffin
- *Professor Branestawm's Treasure Hunt,* Puffin
- *The Peculiar Triumph of Professor Branestawm,* Red Fox
- *Professor Branestawm's Dictionary,* Puffin

About the Author

AUTHOR OF 'RIKKI-TIKKI-TAVI' IN *THE ELEPHANT, THE HARE AND THE BLACK COBRA*

'Rikki-Tikki-Tavi' is a story from *The Jungle Book*, written by Rudyard Kipling in 1894. There are two Jungle Books (*The Second Jungle Book* came out in 1895), both set in India; they tell stories of the jungle animals and a boy called Mowgli, 'the mancub'.

Rudyard Kipling loved India. His parents were English people who were living in Bombay when Rudyard was born in 1865. (They named Rudyard after a lake in Staffordshire where they had met.) Kipling's early years in India, living with his parents and his younger sister, Alice, were very happy.

When he was six, Rudyard and Alice Kipling were sent to live with foster parents in England. They were very unhappy; Kipling called their foster home 'the House of Desolation'. At the age of 12, Rudyard was sent away to a boarding school in Devon. He later wrote a famous school story, called *Stalky and Co.*, based on his experiences there.

When he left school in 1882, Kipling returned to India and started work as a journalist on a daily newspaper. He also wrote poems and stories which were published first in the newspapers and later as books. His work was very successful in India and by the late 1880s it had also become very popular in England.

Kipling married an American and had three children, Josephine, Elsie and John. Josephine died at the age of six; John died as a soldier at the the age of eighteen in the First World War. Kipling lived until 1936. He is buried in Westminster Abbey, in Poet's Corner.

If you enjoyed 'Rikki-Tikki-Tavi' you might like to read more of *The Jungle Books* or the *Just-So Stories*, Kipling's fables about animals.

The Jungle Book has been made into a Disney film and there are lots of retellings of Kipling's stories in print.

Awards
- Kipling was offered many honours and prizes for his work, and he accepted the Nobel Prize for Literature in 1907.

Other books by Rudyard Kipling you might also enjoy:
- *The Jungle Book,* Penguin Popular Classics
- *The Second Jungle Book,* Puffin Classics
- *Just-So Stories,* Penguin Popular Classics

AUTHOR OF *S.T.I.N.K. & CO.*

Though I have written a lot of short stories, *S.T.I.N.K. & Co.* is my first novel. I don't get as much time to read as I would like, but I am rediscovering many of the authors that I loved as a child as I read with my own children. I'm a big fan of Roald Dahl, CS Lewis, Lewis Carroll, Anne Merrick and, of course, JK Rowling. (My favourite adult author is John Irving.) The idea for *S.T.I.N.K. & Co.* came to me while reading a Famous Five adventure story to my daughter. The characters in S.T.I.N.K. are very much 21st century children, and the idea is a kind of parody of the Famous Five. However, both share an incredible knack for getting embroiled in intriguing mysteries and adventures.

When I start writing a story, I generally have a beginning, middle and an end already figured out. But then, as the characters are developed and their personalities come to life, the real telling of the tale begins.

I decided to make Owen the narrator because he is the rational voice of reason. As he describes the ensuing chaos and insanity, the reader can't help but laugh as things spiral out of control. (Well I hope the readers laugh. I wanted to write something that would make people chuckle – a lot!)

I have a number of ideas for possible future S.T.I.N.K. missions. And like the Famous Five, S.T.I.N.K.& Co. would acquire a pet along the way (Stumpy's pet hamster, of course!)

Other books by Rosie McCormick you might also enjoy:
- *Anastasia – The Big Book of the Film*, Golden Books
- *Anastasia – A Mini Story Book*, Golden Books
- *How to Behave like a Princess*, Golden Books
- *In the Dark of the Night*, Golden Books
- *Home is Where You Are*, Golden Books
- *The Lost Princess*, Golden Books
- *Percy the Park Keeper*, Planet 3
- *Six Short Stories for Shooting Stars Series*, Chrysalis/Belitha

About the Author

AUTHOR OF 'THUNDERBALL BADSHAH' IN *RICKY, KARIM AND SPIT NOLAN* **AND** *SHEEKA*

I was born in India and went to universities in Delhi, London and the United States. India is a great inspiration for many of my stories. I go there at least twice a year, to visit my family in New Delhi and to visit other parts of the country.

My story 'Thunderball Badshah' is based in Jaipur, a city I visited recently, where kite-flying is very popular. Kite-flying is a very traditional sport and was always very much a boy's sport when I was growing up. It is very popular in inner cities where rooftops are a substitute for recreation grounds.

When writing this story, I referred to my familiarity with the streets and bazaars of Jaipur and my memories of kite-flying festivals (which usually take place in spring) in order to bring the story and its characters to life.

When I wrote *Sheeka*, I wanted to get away from the authorial voice and didn't want to impose myself on the reader for a change. Deciding to have a 'dog mind' as one of the narrators came to me quite naturally, as I feel that animals (especially intelligent dogs) have thought processes and feelings, even though they don't use human language to express themselves.

I have always loved reading and used to read about six books a week when I was growing up. I have four books on the go at the moment, but when I am on holiday I do my childhood thing and gallop through a book a day!

If you enjoyed reading 'Thunderball Badshah' and *Sheeka*, one of my latest titles could interest you: *The Guru's Family* is set in Coventry and a village in the Punjab.

Awards
- *Dadijan's Carrot Halvah* was listed in Children's Books of the Year 1988.

Other books by Pratima Mitchell you might also enjoy:
- *The Guru's Family,* Hodder Wayland
- *Two Asian Tales, Literacy Land,* Longman
- *Magical Stories from India, Pelican Guided Reading and Writing,* Longman
- *The Tale of a Turban,* Oxford University Press
- *Dance of Shiva,* Hamish Hamilton
- *Dadijan's Carrot Halvah,* Hamish Hamilton

Pratima Mitchell also writes for the *Genre Range* strand of *Literacy Land*, the *Longman Book Project* and *Pelican Guided Reading and Writing*.

AUTHOR OF 'SPIT NOLAN' IN *RICKY, KARIM AND SPIT NOLAN*

Bill Naughton was born in Ireland in 1910. His family moved to England when he was four, and he grew up in Bolton in Lancashire. After he left school, he worked as a coal-bagger and driver for the Co-op and wrote during his spare time. When the Second World War broke out in 1939, he moved to London to work as a civil defence driver.

Bill Naughton's story 'Spit Nolan' comes from a collection of short stories called *The Goalkeeper's Revenge*. These stories, like Bill Naughton's other books for children, are set in the north of England in the 1920s. They are about young people's lives, friendship and sticking together when things get tough.

Bill Naughton wrote for both adults and children. He wrote plays and autobiography, as well as novels and short stories. In the 1950s, his plays began to appear on television and on the radio, and he worked in various teams of writers who produced the scripts for popular TV and radio series.

Bill Naughton loved writing and he wrote a huge amount over his lifetime. He died in 1992 on the Isle of Man, where he lived. The city of Bolton has collected Bill Naughton's papers and published work in an archive because they see him as 'a key figure in English literary life'. Among these papers are five trunks full of Bill Naughton's secret diaries: he has left instructions that these cannot be unlocked until 2015.

If you enjoyed the story Spit Nolan, you should read the other stories in *The Goalkeeper's Revenge*.

Awards
- Bill Naughton won awards for his writing of screenplays, as well as his radio plays and fiction.

Other books by Bill Naughton you might also enjoy:
- *A Dog Called Nelson*, Puffin
- *My Pal Spadger*, Puffin
- *The Goalkeeper's Revenge*, Heinemann
- *Late Night on Watling Street*, Allison & Busby

Linda Newbery

About the Author

AUTHOR OF 'THE UNDERWATER ELEPHANTS' IN *THE ELEPHANT, THE HARE AND THE BLACK COBRA*

The idea behind the story of 'The Underwater Elephants' came from a recent theory that elephants once spent much of their time underwater, using their trunks as breathing tubes. This made me begin to think of a tale, rather like Rudyard Kipling's *Just So Stories*, which would explain this, and why elephants changed their ways to become land animals. I don't usually write stories about talking animals, but this was an exception, and one I really enjoyed writing about!

I enjoy writing for a range of ages. The writing process is much the same, and just as enjoyable, regardless of who the intended audience is. I have often found that one of the best things about writing for younger readers is that you don't have to stick to any one genre, but can write any kind of story you want to try. Most of my books are realistic novels about social issues, for older readers, but some of my most recent writing has led me into different areas.

I think that whatever you're writing, you have to really try and live in that story, live with those characters and see things through their eyes in order to make it work and make it real for the reader. I write stories by asking myself questions such as What if? Why? Who? I wonder whether…? I find that my stories come to me as I am trying to explain the answers to myself. This may take some time as the answers don't necessarily come at once. But the trick is to know which questions to ask, and to keep asking them until you get the answers you are happy with!

You can find a link to my website at www.storystreet.co.uk/streetwise/authors.

Awards
* *The Shell House* was shortlisted for the Guardian Children's Book Award 2003 and the Carnegie Medal 2003.

Other books by Linda Newbery you might also enjoy:
* *Blitz Boys, World War II Flashbacks,* A & C Black
* *Whistling Jack,* Harper Collins, Red Storybook
* *The Shell House,* David Fickling Books
* *The Damage Done,* Scholastic
* *No Way Back,* Orchard
* *Sisterland,* David Fickling Books

AUTHOR OF 'DUCK BOY' IN *BURGLARS, DUCKS AND KISSING FROGS* AND *THE MONKEY'S TALE*

Ever since I was born, I have been surrounded by pets, mostly cats. But, I would have loved a monkey! Nearly all our pets have given us some kind of trouble. In particular I remember one of our cats, Ginger, coming through the cat flap with a whole roast chicken in his jaws! He'd swiped it from someone's kitchen windowsill!

I write in slightly different styles according to the kind of story I'm writing. *The Monkey's Tale* was a little more serious than 'Duck Boy'. You can't make the struggle for survival in winter into comedy! Generally I prefer comedy. I get fed up when everything is deadly serious. I want people to laugh most of the time.

I try my stories out on myself first by reading them out loud. It's a good way to get a feel for them. Sometimes I get one or two adults or children I know to read through and tell me what they think. Almost anything said about my work affects the way I think about my writing, and so it affects the way I actually write.

I often have no idea what I'm going to write next and that's scary. It's great when I have a firm idea about the next book – big sigh of relief! Like most writers I keep notebooks so if I get stuck for ideas I can leaf through the notebooks. Often I will find something that sparks off an idea and off I go again, writing away. I also talk to family and friends when I get stuck. Sometimes I ring another writer, Kaye Umansky, and talk to her. We phone each other up when we get stuck and we have a laugh over the phone and that helps too.

I mostly read animal stories and also a lot of non-fiction when I was young. The non-fiction was mostly historical science – how people did things long ago. I wanted to know how things worked. Nowadays I read all sorts, but mostly adult fiction and travel writers.

You can find a link to my website at www.storystreet.co.uk/streetwise/authors.

Awards
- *My Mum's Going to Explode,* was shortlisted for the 2002 Children's Book Award and won the Nottingham Big 3 Award.
- *Living with Vampires,* won the Short Novel 2001 Sheffield Children's Book Award.
- *Pirate Pandemonium,* won the Short Novel 1998 Sheffield Children's Book Award.
- *The Hundred Mile-an-hour Dog,* won the 1997 Children's Book Award.

Other books by Jeremy Strong you might also enjoy:
- *The Karate Princess and the Last Griffin,* Puffin
- *Krazy Kow Saves the World,* Puffin
- *My Dad's Got an Alligator!,* Puffin
- *There's a Pharaoh in Our Bath!,* Puffin
- *There's a Viking in My Bed!,* Puffin

Jeremy Strong also writes for the *Story Street* and *Info Trail* strands of *Literacy Land*.

About the Author

AUTHOR OF *ALLIGATOR SWAMP*

I grew up in Surrey, went to school in Wimbledon, and university in Cambridge. Since then I've been lucky enough to travel to many different countries. I now spend some of my life in England and some of it in Brazil where my wife, Adriana, comes from.

Alligator Swamp was based on a journey Adriana and I made into the Pantanal several years ago. We camped deep in the swamp with a guide called Murilo Reis. He had grown up on a farm nearby and, like Pedrinho, knew each twist of the rivers and the names of every bird that flew by. We stayed at a camp he'd set up on a sandy riverbank. There were three alligators living along that stretch of river. They were wild but Murilo used to feed them fish, talk to them and give them shoulder massages (!) just like Pedrinho.

We waded through deep water, crossed stretches of forest and fished for piranhas just like Ant does in the book. So, unbelievable as it might all seem, the alligators, the piranhas and the setting of the story are completely real.

Once we passed a man trying to kill an anaconda with a stick. Murilo shouted at him and told him to leave the snake alone. But I didn't actually see the alligator poaching that comes into my book. People talked about that. It is illegal in Brazil, but very easy to do. The poachers stun the alligators with lamps, then shoot them. To write that part of the story I had to do some research. I contacted two Brazilian environmental scientists who answered my questions. Adriana has an uncle who once ran a farm near the Pantanal and he gave me details for the scenes around the farmhouse.

I'd love to think that some of you readers will have a go at writing an adventure story of your own. My advice would be to set your story in a place that you know. It doesn't have to be exotic. You can have adventures anywhere. It's the characters you invent and the tests that you give them that really bring a story to life. So spend plenty of time "getting to know" your characters. And I'd make sure you map out your story before you start writing. When I set off into a book I like to have a good ending planned and a clear idea of how I'm going to get there. But, like many writers, I'm a wanderer and I don't always take the route I thought I would or reach the ending I expected!

Other books by Sean Taylor you might also like:

* *Carnival King*, Oxford University Press
* *The Huge and Horrible Beast*, Oxford University Press
* *Silly Stories from Here, There and Everywhere*, Heinemann
* *Headfirst into the Porridge*, Rigby
* *The Woodcutter and the Bear*, Rigby

AUTHOR OF *PRINCE PANTYHOSE*

The idea for *Prince Pantyhose* came to me one day when I was listening to a phone-in radio programme. People were discussing Prince Charles, and one very passionate woman rang in to say that it wasn't fair to keep criticising him as he had 'a very hard life' and she didn't think many people would want to change places with him. That got me thinking ... how hard was Prince Charles' life compared, say, with the life of someone living on one of our council estates? How would Prince Charles like it if he were suddenly whisked off to a council estate? How would someone from a council estate feel if he were whisked off to Prince Charles' country estate?

The idea of a prince changing places with a pauper is a classical fairy tale situation, and that is why I set the book in 'once upon a time' and told it in the style of a fairy tale. Does Prince Pantyhose get his just deserts? Has the story got a moral? That's up to the reader to decide!

Because I usually write about ordinary, everyday things – things that are going on all around me, all of the time – I never seem to run out of ideas. When I get an idea I put it into the computer inside my head and every now and again I click onto it and start daydreaming. Bit by bit, a storyline emerges and I get to know my characters, until in the end I feel ready to get to grips with the actual writing. While I'm actually writing, part of me is thinking of the reader. Will this interest the reader? Will the reader understand what I'm saying? Part of me is thinking as my characters would think, and part of me is sitting back controlling it all. It's all very complex!

You can find a link to my website at www.storystreet.co.uk/streetwise/authors.

Awards
- *Plague* won the Lancashire Book Award in 1990.
- *Whistle and I'll Come* won the Stockton Children's Award.
- *Bad Alice* was on the Guardian Children's Book Award long list.
- *Becky Bananas* was shortlisted for the Sheffield Children's Award.

Other books by Jean Ure you might enjoy:
- *Daisy May,* Harper Collins
- *Fruit & Nutcase,* Harper Collins
- *Becky Bananas,* Harper Collins
- *Shrinking Violet,* Harper Collins
- *Dazzling Danny,* Harper Collins

About the Author

AUTHOR OF 'BROWN HARE AND THE FOX' IN *THE ELEPHANT, THE HARE AND THE BLACK COBRA*

One cold morning in Clare I woke very early, and walked alone by the side of a lake. Why? I was on holiday there with my children, and that morning I just felt like being out on my own, that's why. The last thing I was expecting was that I'd find a story ... but I did.

Something moved in a field by the lake, then was still, seemed to quiver, then moved again quickly and was gone ... *hoppity-hoppity-hop* into the long grass. I stood very still, and watched. It reappeared, further up the field. Quiver ... *hoppity-hoppity-hop, this way and this way and this way and that* ... gone again, disappearing into the rocks and furze.

I'd just met Brown Hare, and I knew she was a *story* but I didn't know what sort of story. The words 'hoppity' and 'this way and that' were there from the beginning, tangled with the image, the remoteness, the dark green of the field and the bright light of dawn on the lake.

Sometimes people think writers are lazy, all that standing about in fields, doing nothing. But the *nothing* can quickly become *something* and churn about in the head, till the day comes when it wants to be written. It was years later that this one resurfaced. *Hoppity-hoppity-hop* and my writing mind was back in Clare, by the lake ... though in real life I was at my desk, in the stone barn by the sea, where I write my stories.

I started with the hare, and the cold morning in Clare ... that *ryhmes* ... and I thought of the beauty of the setting, with the lake flashing in the cold sunlight and ... and ... what then?

That's the trouble with being a writer. The words can be interesting, sometimes beautiful, but something has to *happen* to make it a story. There have to be characters in it ... someone to see Brown Hare, and think 'hoppity-hoppity-hoppity-hop'. Go with just the words, and you have a short descriptive poem that catches a beautiful moment. Stories need more than that. They need people, conflict, action, drama.

Off goes my mind *this way and this way and this way and that* ....

Hoppity-hoppity-hoppity-hop, that's how this story was written.

Awards
- *Can't You Sleep Little Bear?* won the Smarties Prize in 1988 and the Kate Greenaway Award in 1988.
- *Starry Night* was shortlisted for the Guardian Young Fiction Award.
- *Frankie's Story* was shortlisted for the Carnegie Award.

Other books by Martin Waddell you might also enjoy:
- *The Life and Loves of Zoe T Curly,* Walker Books
- *The Kidnapping of Susie Q,* Walker Books
- *Shooting Star,* Walker Books
- *The Orchard Book of Ghostly Stories,* Orchard
- *The Dump Gang,* Walker Books
- *Fred the Angel,* Walker Books

Martin Waddell also writes for the *Genre Range* strand of *Literacy Land* and the *Longman Book Project*.